Adulting 101

Life Skills for Growing Up

Everything school didn't teach you about life, made simple.

Adulting 101: Life Skills for Growing Up

This book was a labor of love, with every detail: writing,
cover design, editing, and layout.
by Aaron B. Kershaw.

Language: English
ISBN: 979-8-90345-200-2

Format: Paperback

Adulting 101

Life Skills for Growing Up

First published in 2025.
Revised trade edition published in 2026 by
BuildingBlocs Publishing, Inc.

Raleigh, North Carolina 27606

Printed in the United States of America

-- 4 --

Adulting 101: Life Skills for Growing Up

-- 9 --

Adulting 101: Life Skills for Growing Up

Introduction: Life Skills, Not Just for Home Economics Class

Hey, future life ninja. You've probably heard it a million times, "Get your life together!", but no one's really telling you *how*, right? Well, Uncle Aaron's got you covered. This isn't some boring life manual full of stale advice and buzzwords. Nope. We're diving into real talk: how to handle money, not burn your kitchen down, manage your time like a boss, and even how to communicate like a human in a world full of emojis and DMs.

Why life skills matter? Because being able to "adult" properly is your golden ticket to freedom. But spoiler alert, it's not all about having a 9-to-5 and knowing how to pay taxes. It's about mastering the basics so you can own life, avoid unnecessary freakouts, and still have fun while doing it.

This book? It's your cheat code to get ahead, whether that means budgeting without living off instant noodles or assembling IKEA furniture without losing your mind. We're going to break down all the adulting things you never got taught in school, in a way that doesn't feel like an extra homework assignment. Think of this as your guide to becoming an actual functional human, minus the boring bits.

By the end of this book, you won't just survive adulting, you'll thrive at it. We'll tackle everything from mastering your money, to balancing time, cooking meals that won't kill you, keeping your social media presence from haunting you, and even the basics of networking like a pro (spoiler: it's not just LinkedIn). Plus, we'll sprinkle in some humor, because let's face it, adulting without a sense of humor is a nightmare.

So, buckle up. We're about to dive into life skills you'll actually use. Ready to level up? Let's do this.

Why Life Skills Matter

Okay, imagine this: You're 23, living on your own, and it's all going well until, BAM, you burn your dinner, forget to pay your utility bill, and realize you have no clue how taxes work. Now, you could call your parents in a panic, but at some point, they're going to stop answering your "how do I adult?" texts. That's where life skills come in, my friend.

Life skills are like cheat codes for the game of life. You think they don't matter until you're staring at an Ikea bookshelf wondering if it's a puzzle or furniture, or worse, you're eating cereal for the fourth night in a row because you never learned how to boil pasta without it turning into mush. Life skills save you from these minor catastrophes and set you up for the bigger challenges like, oh, I don't know, getting a job or making sure you don't bounce a rent check.

Being good with money, time, communication, and basic life tasks is your secret weapon to winning at adulthood. It's like having the best loadout in a video game, you're equipped, confident, and ready for whatever comes your way. Plus, knowing how to manage your life is what gives you freedom. Want to live in another city? Cool, you won't need anyone to babysit you through basic tasks like making sure the lights stay on. Want to start your own side hustle? Well, you're going to need to manage your time and money, or that dream will die fast.

Life skills let you roll with the punches, because, trust me, life *will* throw them. You'll be the person who's not just surviving but thriving. It's about self-sufficiency and knowing that no matter what life tosses at you, you've got the knowledge to handle it. It's freedom, baby, and who doesn't want that?

Uncle Aaron's Reality Check on Adulting

Here's the truth no one tells you: adulting is not this magical moment where you wake up one day and suddenly know how to fold a fitted sheet, pay your taxes, and make lasagna from scratch. Nope. Adulting is a slow, messy process that's 90% learning from failure and 10% hoping nobody notices how clueless you are. And guess what? That's *normal.*

When you turn 18 or 21 or even 30, you don't suddenly unlock the mysteries of life. You don't get an "adulting manual" (and if you do, I'd like a refund on mine). Instead, you get a lot of trial and error. The good news is messing up is how you learn. The first time I tried to do laundry; I ended up dyeing my white clothes a lovely shade of baby blue. The second time, I didn't use enough detergent, and my clothes smelled like a wet dog. But by the third time? I was a laundry ninja.

Here's another shocker: adults, the ones you see looking all put together, are faking it too. Everyone's just winging it, some people are just better at hiding the chaos. The trick isn't about becoming a perfect adult. It's about becoming a *capable* one. Learn the basics, figure out how to troubleshoot when things go sideways, and most importantly, keep your sense of humor. You're going to mess up, so laugh about it, learn, and move on. No one really cares that you accidentally melted a spatula on the stove or burned your first attempt at dinner (trust me, we've all been there).

Adulting is about resilience and adaptability. The more skills you pick up along the way, the easier it gets. But don't sweat it. You're not behind, you're exactly where you need to be, somewhere between 'I got this' and 'What the hell am I doing?' And guess what? That's where everyone else is too. So, let's get to learning, laughing, and mastering the art of not having it all together, but making it work anyway.

Chapter 1: Financial Literacy

Don't Let Money Manage You

Let me paint a picture, first paycheck, 16 years old, feeling rich enough to buy the world. Two weeks later? My bank account was emptier than a vending machine after a high school basketball game. I didn't even remember half the purchases. That's how fast money can ghost you if you're not paying attention.

Money can either be your best friend or your worst enemy. If you don't get a handle on it early, you'll find yourself scrambling, living paycheck to paycheck, and wondering where it all went (hint: those spontaneous Amazon buys might be a clue). In this chapter, we're going to tackle how to take control of your cash, manage your money smartly, and set yourself up to avoid any financial panic attacks. It's about becoming financially literate without feeling like you need to turn into a Wall Street whiz kid.

1. The Basics: Money In, Money Out

Think of money like calories. If you take in more than you burn, it sticks to you. If you spend more than you earn, it sticks to your debt. Neither is comfortable, both are preventable.

Also, the first time you actually track every dollar, you'll feel like you just opened your fridge and found three-month-old leftovers. Disgusting, but enlightening.

Let's start with a simple equation: **income vs. expenses**. That's the foundation of every financial situation. Income is what comes in, whether it's from a job, freelance gig, or side hustle, and expenses are what flows out. If you spend more than you make, well, we have a problem, Houston. But keeping things balanced isn't as hard as it seems, and it doesn't mean you need to cut out all fun. Instead, it's about being conscious of your spending habits and making sure your money is working for you, not against you.

Here's how it works:

Track Your Spending: Start by figuring out where your money is going. You'd be surprised how much you're dropping on small, everyday expenses (hello, Starbucks).

Build a Spending Log: Use apps like Mint, or just go old-school with a notebook, to write down every time you spend money. After a month, review it. This exercise is like a financial slap in the face; it forces you to confront your spending habits head-on. You might not like what you see, but that's the first step to fixing it.

Next, let's talk about your **needs** vs. **wants**. Netflix? Probably a want (though, to be honest, in this day and age, we can argue it's a need). Rent and groceries? Needs. You need to identify these clearly. Knowing what's essential helps you prioritize your spending.

2. Creating a Budget That Doesn't Suck

A budget isn't a prison sentence; it's your security detail. It's there to keep you out of trouble, not lock you in a cell.

If the word "budget" makes you want to nap, rename it something cool like "Freedom Plan" or "Operation Stop Being Broke." Works wonders.

The word "budget" gets a bad rap but hear me out. Budgeting isn't about depriving yourself of everything fun, it's about making sure you get to have fun without being broke the last week of every month. The magic formula? Try the **50/30/20 rule**:

- 50% on needs (housing, food, utilities)

- 30% on wants (entertainment, dining out, hobbies)

- 20% on savings and debt repayment (because in the future, you will appreciate that emergency fund).

This rule keeps things simple, but here's the kicker: the reality today is that housing costs have skyrocketed in many areas. In cities and regions where rent or mortgage payments are eating up more than 50% of your income, sticking to the 50/30/20 rule can feel like trying to fit a square peg in a round hole. So, what do you do when your rent alone blows the 50% mark?

How to Modify Your Budget for Today's Reality

If your rent's eating more than half your paycheck, you're not financially reckless, you're just living in 2025. This isn't about shame, it's about strategy.

Don't cling to some internet rule like it's the Ten Commandments. Your budget is a living thing, like a houseplant. Adjust the care, or it dies.

In today's expensive housing market, you may need to adjust your budget to reflect real life. If housing costs are closer to 60% (or more) of your income, don't panic. This isn't a financial death sentence, it just means you have to adapt. You can still budget effectively, even when your expenses don't fit neatly into traditional categories.

Here's how you can tweak the formula:

- 60% on needs (because housing is eating a larger chunk of the pie, rent, food, utilities all count here).

- 20% on wants (yes, you can still have some fun, but you may need to cut back on non-essentials like frequent dining out or new clothes).

- 20% on savings and debt repayment (it's important to keep saving, even if it feels hard right now, more on that in a moment).

If saving 20% feels impossible, aim for at least 10-15%. Something is better than nothing, and the key is to stay consistent. You can adjust and gradually increase your savings as your financial situation improves. Budgets are living documents; they're meant to flex with your circumstances. Keep tweaking it as your income and expenses change. The main goal is to ensure that you don't fall into the habit of overspending in the "wants" category just because housing is high. Keeping that balance means you'll still be able to build a cushion for your future.

3. Savings 101: Why Saving is So Important

Saving money isn't about hoarding it like a dragon in a cave. It's about building a trampoline so when life drops you, you bounce instead of splat.

And yes, "future you" is watching everything you do right now. Make them proud, or at least not furious.

Saving isn't just for rich people or those planning to buy a yacht (though, hey, if that's your goal, go for it). It's for anyone who wants to avoid living paycheck to paycheck or panicking every time something unexpected happens. Think of saving as your financial safety net, it's what stands between you and a full-blown crisis when life throws you a curveball. Saving money doesn't just protect your finances, it protects your mental health too. After all, no one likes the stress of an empty bank account.

Why You Need an Emergency Fund

Your emergency fund is the friend who shows up at 3 a.m. when your car won't start. You don't think about them much… until you really need them.

Also, if you think "I'll just use my credit card in an emergency," remember debt is not a rescue plan, it's a delayed disaster.

Life has a way of being unpredictable. Your car breaks down, you get a medical bill, your laptop dies the night before a big project, these things happen. That's where your emergency fund comes in.

It's there to save the day when something unexpected hits, and trust me, it will happen eventually. Having an emergency fund gives you peace of mind knowing that you can handle life's hiccups without resorting to credit cards or loans, which could snowball into even bigger problems.

Even if you start small, the key is to build up to at least $500 to $1000. That might not cover every disaster, but it's enough to take care of many common emergencies. Over time, aim to save 3-6 months of living expenses. I know that sounds daunting, but it's about progress, not perfection. Start by putting away a little bit each month, eventually, it adds up.

Why Long-Term Savings Matter

Compound interest is like that one snowball you throw down a hill, it starts small, but by the time it gets to the bottom, it can crush a car.

The trick? Start rolling it now, even if it's tiny.

Think about this: future you is going to have needs, too. Whether it's buying a house, going on vacation, or just ensuring you can retire without living off cat food (I'm exaggerating...sort of), long-term savings are essential. It's easy to focus on immediate expenses and let future goals take a back seat, but the sooner you start saving, the better off you'll be in the long run.

Why? Because of compound interest, the magical process where your money starts earning interest, and then that interest earns interest. It's like getting a snowball rolling downhill. Over time, it gets bigger and bigger without you having to do much. But here's the catch, it only works if you start early. Even small contributions to savings accounts or investment funds now can grow significantly by the time you're ready to cash in.

Whether your goal is to retire comfortably, travel the world, or just have some peace of mind, long-term savings are the foundation for all of those dreams. Future-you will be very grateful for any steps you take now.

How to Build Your Savings

Automate your savings so you never have to think about it. Out of sight, out of temptation.

If it's not in your checking account, you can't spend it at 2 a.m. on something you don't remember buying the next day.

Automate it. Most banks allow you to set up automatic transfers to savings, which takes the stress (and the temptation to spend) out of the equation. Even if it's just $20 per paycheck, that's better than nothing. Over time, you can increase that amount as you get used to living with less spending money.

The trick is to treat savings like a non-negotiable expense, just like rent or groceries. You'll adjust your lifestyle to make it work, and in the end, it'll give you much more freedom.

Wrapping It Up: Why Saving is Your Superpower

Saving isn't sexy in the moment, but financial freedom is the best-looking outfit you'll ever wear.

Think of every saved dollar as a tiny soldier fighting for your future.

Saving money might not seem glamorous, but it's one of the most powerful tools you have in your financial toolkit. Whether you're building an emergency fund to cover life's unexpected disasters or putting money away for long-term goals like a house, a vacation, or retirement, saving gives you options. It allows you to navigate life without constantly worrying about how to pay the bills.

Think of saving as a way to buy yourself peace of mind and future freedom. You don't need to have it all figured out right now, but starting with small, consistent habits will set you up for success. Whether you're working with the traditional 50/30/20 budget or a more flexible approach based on today's reality, the key is to keep moving forward. Every dollar saved is a step toward a better, more secure future.

4. Credit Cards: Friend or Foe?

A credit card is like fire; it can cook your dinner or burn down your house. The difference is how you handle it.

Never swipe in a mood. Happy, sad, stressed, all dangerous times for plastic.

Credit cards have a bit of a split personality. On one hand, they're a great tool for building credit and handling emergencies. On the other hand, they can trap you in a cycle of debt faster than you can say "minimum payment." The trick is understanding how to use them smartly.

Here's the golden rule: **Don't spend money you don't have**. A credit card isn't free money; it's borrowed cash that you'll need to pay back. If you carry a balance and only pay the minimum, interest will rack up, and suddenly, that $50 shirt is costing you $75 (or more).

The smarter way to use a credit card:

- **Pay off the balance in full** every month if you can.

- **Don't max it out**, try to keep your credit utilization below 30% of your limit.

- Use it like you would cash, if you wouldn't spend $50 in cash, don't charge it on your card.

Used wisely, credit cards can help you build credit, which is essential for things like getting a loan, renting an apartment, or even some jobs. Used recklessly, they can lead to a financial nightmare. So tread carefully!

5. Building Credit and Why You Should Care

Your credit score is your financial dating profile. A good one gets you attention and better offers. A bad one? Let's just say… fewer swipes.

You might be thinking, "Why do I care about credit?" Well, here's the deal: your credit score is like your financial reputation. A high score means you're seen as reliable, which translates into better interest rates on loans, more rental options, and even job opportunities. A low score? Not so much. Building a good credit score is like planting seeds that'll grow into financial benefits later in life.

Here's how to build good credit:

- **Pay your bills on time**, this is the biggest factor in your score.

- **Keep your credit card balances low**, don't max them out.

- **Don't close old accounts**, the length of your credit history matters, so keep those older accounts open even if you don't use them.

And no, you don't need a perfect score to reap the benefits. Anything above 700 is considered good, and above 800 is excellent. The key is consistency, build good habits now, and your future self will thank you.

6. Loans and Debt: Handle with Care

A loan is like a pet, if you can't afford to feed it, you shouldn't bring it home.

Also, read the terms twice. Once for the numbers, once for the fine print they hope you'll ignore.

At some point, you may need a loan, whether it's for college, a car, or even a house down the road. Loans aren't inherently bad, but they come with responsibility. The key is understanding how much debt you can handle and what it's going to cost you in the long run.

Interest rates are sneaky. Borrow $10,000 at 5%, and over time, you'll pay back more than you borrowed. Understand the terms of any loan before you sign the dotted line. And don't borrow more than you can comfortably pay back, trust me, you don't want to be stuck with loan payments that eat up your paycheck.

Wrapping It Up: Money Doesn't Have to Be Scary

The goal isn't to make you rich overnight, it's to make you unbreakable over time.

Start now, start small, but start. Because tomorrow shows up faster than you think.

Money doesn't have to be stressful. By understanding the basics, how to budget, save, manage credit, and handle debt, you're taking control of your financial future. You don't need to be a finance expert to handle your money like a pro. Start with small changes, build good habits, and over time, you'll watch your money grow and your stress shrink.

Adulting is hard enough without financial headaches, so take the time now to get on top of your money. Once you do, you'll be able to live with more freedom, fewer worries, and a lot more confidence. Let's go get that financial freedom, one smart decision at a time.

Chapter 2: Cooking Skills

From Ramen to Real Food

First rule of adulting: learn to feed yourself something that didn't come in a Styrofoam cup. It's cheaper than therapy, sexier than a gym membership, and keeps you from living off granola bars because you "forgot" to grocery shop.

Listen, knowing how to cook isn't just about surviving, it's a superpower that'll score you major points with future roommates, dates, or even yourself when you realize you don't have to rely on delivery every night. Whether you're a guy wanting to impress someone with a home-cooked meal or a girl tired of microwaving last night's leftovers, learning a few tricks in the kitchen is going to pay off big time. Plus, you know what they say: "The fastest way to someone's heart is through their stomach." Trust me, it's true.

Cooking for Survival: The Bare Minimum

The smoke detector is not your kitchen timer. If it's going off, that's not applause.

Let's get one thing straight, knowing how to make a decent meal could save your social life. You don't need to master gourmet dishes to impress someone, but knowing how to cook something edible? Yeah, that'll make you stand out. Whether you're cooking for yourself or trying to impress a date, the bar is low, people. You're already ahead of the curve if you know how to fry an egg or boil some pasta without setting off the smoke detector.

The Staples:

Eggs, pasta, and grilled cheese are like the holy trinity of cheap eats. Nail these, and you're basically the Gordon Ramsay of broke twenty-somethings.

- **Eggs**: Universally loved by both guys and girls. Fried, scrambled, boiled, it doesn't matter. Eggs are cheap, versatile, and full of protein, which is good news for the gym bros trying to bulk up or anyone trying to eat healthy. Plus, if you can whip up a killer breakfast, you're automatically more dateable. I don't make the rules.

- **Pasta**: Whether you're impressing someone with your "Italian roots" (fake or real), pasta is the ultimate go-to. It's easy, quick, and hard to mess up. Grab a jar of sauce, throw in some meat or veggies, and suddenly, you're a chef.

- **Grilled Cheese**: Okay, hear me out, there's something magical about grilled cheese. It's the ultimate comfort food, and if you add a little twist (like some avocado or bacon), you've taken it to the next level. Trust me, it's a crowd-pleaser.

Guys, you may think cooking is "girly," but news flash: nothing gets you more brownie points than knowing how to handle yourself in the kitchen. Girls, it's about time we leave behind the idea that cooking is only for special occasions. Learning the basics is a game-changer in keeping you fed without resorting to takeout. Everyone wins here.

Easy, Healthy Meals That Don't Suck

Healthy cooking isn't code for "rabbit food." It's code for "I can still button my jeans after a weekend of bad decisions."

Here's the thing: whether you're hitting the gym or just trying to stay in shape, eating healthy doesn't mean choking down salads like a rabbit. You can still eat food that's *actually good* while keeping it on the healthy side. And guess what? Being able to whip up a healthy meal shows you've got your life together, which is lowkey attractive, just saying.

Simple, Healthy Recipes:

Stir-fry is just "throw stuff in a pan and pretend it's intentional." Tacos are the love language of the hungry. And sheet-pan chicken? That's the closest you'll get to adult magic.

- **Stir-Fry**: Veggies, protein, and a sauce that doesn't come from a fast-food packet. It's quick, customizable, and perfect for anyone wanting to stay fit or just look like they know what they're doing. Tip: it's also great for when you're cooking for someone else, impress them with a simple yet classy meal that looks way more complicated than it is.

- **Tacos**: Forget Taco Bell. Homemade tacos are where it's at, and it's a perfect date-night dish, easy to assemble and fun to eat. Plus, you can load them up with fresh ingredients and impress your date with your "healthy" food choices.

- **One-Pot Chicken and Veggies**: Want to sound like a meal-prepping genius? Toss some chicken and vegetables on a baking sheet with a few seasonings, roast it all in the oven, and suddenly you've got a healthy dinner that'll last a few days. You can swap in different veggies or sauces to keep it interesting without much effort.

And here's the kicker, guys, the idea that you know how to cook a decent meal without resorting to protein shakes or microwave meals will blow people's minds. Girls, taking control of your nutrition without ordering overpriced salads? Game changer.

Meal Prepping Without Losing Your Mind

Meal prep is basically future-you leaving present-you a love note in Tupperware form.

You've probably seen those fitness influencers showing off their 20 Tupperware containers for the week, and while that level of meal prepping is next level, you don't need to go that far. Meal prepping is all about making life easier, so you're not scrambling to figure out dinner after a long day. Plus, showing someone, you've got meals ready for the week? Major responsible adult points.

How to Meal Prep Like a Pro:

Keep it simple. Nobody needs seven different dinners for the week. This isn't a cooking show; it's survival with a side of style.

Step 1: Pick a Day: Meal prep doesn't have to take hours, dedicate a couple of hours once a week, usually on Sundays, to batch cook a few meals. You don't need to be making gourmet meals either. Think simple and repeatable.

Step 2: Choose 2-3 Recipes: Make it easy on yourself. Don't try to cook seven different meals. Stick to two or three recipes that you like (and that don't require a ton of ingredients). Things like pasta, stir-fry, and sheet-pan chicken are easy to prep in bulk.

Step 3: Pack It Up: Invest in a few containers and portion out your meals. You'll save time during the week, avoid spending money on fast food, and it's one less thing you have to think about after a long day.

Why Meal Prep is a Win:

The only thing better than a fridge full of ready-to-eat meals is not having to talk to anyone while you eat them.

Saves Time: You cook once and eat for days. No more "What's for dinner?" panic at 7 p.m. when you're hangry and considering whether cold pizza is a viable option.

Saves Money: Eating out constantly gets expensive. Meal prepping means you've got homemade meals ready to go at a fraction of the cost. Imagine what you could do with all that extra cash.

Impressive AF: Let's be real, showing someone, you're organized enough to meal prep automatically makes you look like you've got your life together. Whether it's a date or just friends, being the one who has meals prepped shows a whole new level of maturity.

Guys, knowing how to meal prep shows you're disciplined and know how to take care of yourself, there's nothing more attractive than that. Girls, you'll feel like a boss knowing you're in control of your food choices without spending all your money on takeout. Everyone wins.

Eating Out vs. Cooking at Home: The Real Deal

Every time you order takeout, that's a chunk of your paycheck saying goodbye forever. Cook at home and you'll have enough leftover for Netflix and snacks.

Let's break it down: cooking at home isn't just for saving money; it's a power move. Sure, grabbing dinner out with friends or ordering Uber Eats feels easy, but when you stack it up, cooking at home is cheaper, healthier, and, dare I say, sexier. Picture this: you invite someone over and actually cook for them. Boom. Instant cool points. Now compare that to ordering takeout and hoping the delivery guy shows up on time.

Cost Breakdown:

Eating out five times a week is basically a car payment you're making to DoorDash.

Eating Out: You drop $15-20 on a meal without even realizing it. Multiply that by five meals a week, and suddenly you've blown through $100, money you probably didn't even know you were spending. Add drinks, and you're talking even more.

Cooking at Home: For the same $100, you can buy groceries to make enough meals for the entire week, breakfast, lunch, and dinner. That's **$3-5 per meal**. Even if you're cooking something a little fancier, it's still cheaper and healthier than most restaurant options.

Health Factor:

Restaurants don't care about your macros, they care if you come back for dessert.

Eating Out: Even if you're trying to eat healthy at a restaurant, you're probably getting a lot of hidden fats, sugars, and salt. Restaurant food is designed to taste good, not necessarily to be good for you. That salad? Drenched in dressing. Those grilled veggies? Cooked in butter.

Cooking at Home: You're in control of what goes into your meals. You can opt for lean proteins, healthy fats, and whole grains without the hidden calorie bombs. Plus, knowing how to cook a healthy meal? That's some next-level adulting.

Final Thoughts: Cooking is Cool

Cooking for someone is like a first date and a magic trick rolled into one. They show up hungry, you wave a spatula, and boom , they're impressed.

If you take away anything from this chapter, let it be this: knowing how to cook is a game-changer. It's cheaper, healthier, and gives you the freedom to eat what you want, when you want. And hey, if impressing your friends, family, or a potential partner is part of the deal, why not embrace it? Because let's face it, there's something seriously attractive about someone who knows their way around a kitchen.

Whether you're prepping meals for the week, trying to cook something a little healthier, or just want to step up your game, learning how to cook is an investment that'll pay off in more ways than one. So grab a pan, find a recipe, and get started. Your wallet, your waistline, and maybe even your love life will thank you.

Chapter 3: Time Management and Goal Setting

Keep Calm and Get It Done

You're not actually "too busy." You're just letting your time leak out the side like a cheap takeout container. Patch the leaks, and suddenly you've got hours you didn't know you had.

We've all been there, staring at the mountain of stuff we need to do while somehow still finding time to scroll through endless TikToks of people who are *way* more productive than us. Whether you're trying to keep up with classes, work, or figuring out how to make time for Netflix marathons *and* the gym, it feels like there's never enough time. But don't worry, I've got some tricks to help you manage your time without losing your mind, or your social life.

How to Manage Your Time Before It Manages You

If you don't run your day, your day will run you… usually face-first into a deadline you forgot about.

Let's be real, most of us (guys and girls alike) aren't born with great time management skills. We're either procrastinating professionals or we've got a to-do list so long it could double as a novel. The secret isn't trying to become some time-blocking robot, it's about working smarter, not harder.

The Time Audit:

This might sound boring, but you can't fix something if you don't know it's broken, right? Spend a day (or two) tracking everything you do. Yes, that means logging those 45 minutes of doomscrolling or that hour you spent watching dog videos. By the end of it, you'll probably be shocked at how much time you're wasting. Guys, this is your wake-up call to get off the Xbox, and girls, yes, your makeup tutorials on YouTube are eating up your whole morning.

To-Do Lists, But Make Them Work for You:

Forget about the endless to-do lists that make you want to give up before you start. Keep it simple, just write down the 3-5 most important things you need to get done today. Nothing else. No one's saying you need to solve world peace, just focus on today's stuff. Girls, you can balance your planner aesthetic *and* productivity, and guys, trust me, writing things down doesn't make you less cool. It makes you less likely to forget to do laundry before your last clean shirt is history.

Time Blocking: The MVP of Time Management

Time blocking is a game-changer. Pick chunks of time for specific tasks. It's like setting up appointments with yourself to get stuff done, 10 AM to 11 AM: homework; 3 PM to 4 PM: hit the gym.

Guys, this'll give you actual time to finish that FIFA tournament without skipping responsibilities, and girls, it's the secret to squeezing in self-care, classes, and social life. Time blocking turns chaos into control.

Setting Realistic Goals: That Don't Feel Like Homework

A goal you secretly hate will die in under a week. Make it something you actually want, not something you think will impress strangers.

Goals are great until you realize the ones you set sound amazing but feel impossible. The key? Make them bite-sized and realistic so you don't want to quit two days in. This goes for everyone, whether your goal is hitting the gym more, saving money for a killer vacation, or finally learning how to cook something other than toast.

The SMART Goal Method (AKA The Life Hack)

SMART goals aren't sexy, but they work. It's like turning your dream into IKEA instructions, follow the steps, and you actually get the thing you wanted instead of a wobbly mess.

Boys, girls, it's time to get strategic. SMART goals aren't some corporate nonsenses, they actually work. Make your goals:

- **Specific**: Not "I want to work out more," but "I'll work out three times a week."

- **Measurable**: Track it, like seeing gains at the gym or getting your grades up.

- **Achievable**: If you haven't been to the gym in a year, don't aim to go daily. Start with baby steps.

- **Relevant**: Make sure it matters to *you*.

- **Time-bound**: Set a deadline, otherwise, it'll stay on your "someday" list forever.

Girls, this means setting clear goals that don't feel overwhelming, and guys, it's about seeing actual progress instead of getting frustrated and quitting after two days.

Small Wins Add Up:

Think of it like Lego bricks. One brick looks like nothing. A hundred bricks later, you've got a castle.

Listen, the quickest way to fail is to think you need to do everything at once. You don't go from couch potato to marathon runner overnight, right? Take it step by step. If you're trying to save money, start by skipping the $7 latte. If you're aiming for better grades, set aside one extra hour of study time a week. Small wins build up, and before you know it, you're crushing your goals.

Beating Procrastination: How to Get Off TikTok and Actually Do Stuff

You don't have a motivation problem, you have a "starting" problem. Fix that, and everything else follows.

Procrastination: the universal enemy of productivity. We all do it, whether you're avoiding homework, workouts, or that project you've been putting off for weeks. The good news? You can trick your brain into getting things done without it feeling like torture.

The 5-Minute Rule:

The next time you feel like putting something off (again), tell yourself you only have to do it for **five minutes**. That's it. After five minutes, if you still hate it, stop. But here's the secret: once you start, you'll probably keep going because the hardest part is just *starting*. Guys, this means no more convincing yourself "I'll do it later." Girls, you can absolutely use this to finally start that essay you've been dreading.

Eat the Frog:

No, I'm not telling you to actually eat a frog (unless you're into that). It's a phrase that means tackling your least favorite task first thing in the morning. Got a huge paper due? Knock out the first page before lunch. Dreading laundry day? Throw a load in as soon as you wake up. Once the worst task is done, the rest of your day feels easy. Boys, get that assignment or errand out of the way early, and girls, you'll feel like you're already winning by 9 AM.

Reward Yourself: (Because You Deserve It)

Here's the trick to making productivity less miserable, reward yourself. Once you've tackled a big task, give yourself something to look forward to. Maybe it's grabbing a coffee, watching an episode of your favorite show, or taking a break to scroll Instagram. Whatever it is, make it worth it. Guys, no gaming until the work is done, and girls, the TikTok dance tutorials can wait until after the assignment is submitted.

Final Thoughts: It's About Progress, Not Perfection

Perfect is a fantasy. Progress is a paycheck. Collect enough of them, and you'll be shocked at how far you've come.

At the end of the day, time management and goal setting aren't about being perfect, they're about making progress. You don't need to have your entire life planned down to the minute, but taking control of your time means more freedom to do the things you actually want to do. Boys, mastering time management means you'll have time for the gym, gaming, and hanging out with friends. Girls, it's the secret to balancing school, self-care, and your social life without burning out.

Take it one step at a time, set realistic goals, and tackle procrastination head-on. Time is on your side; you just have to manage it like a boss. Let's get stuff done!

-- 43 --

Chapter 4: Basic Home Maintenance

Channel Your Inner DIY Guru

Owning basic home repair skills isn't just a money-saver, it's a confidence booster. The day you fix something without calling for help, you'll feel like you've unlocked a secret adulting level.

Welcome to adulting, where things break unexpectedly, and knowing how to fix them can save you a ton of money, and stress. Whether you've just moved into your first apartment or you're settling into your own house, mastering the basics of home repair is a life skill that's going to make you a certified pro. Don't worry, you don't need to be a handyman (or woman) to handle most of the common issues that pop up. But with a little know-how and a well-stocked toolkit, you'll be ready to tackle just about anything.

Knowing how to fix stuff doesn't just save you money, it makes you look like a total boss. So whether you're a guy who wants to flex his DIY muscles or a girl who's tired of waiting for someone else to handle the "manly" stuff, it's time to dive in.

The Ultimate DIY Toolkit: The Must-Have Tools for Any Home

Think of this like building your superhero utility belt, only instead of fighting crime, you're fighting loose screws and leaky faucets.

Alright, let's start with the foundation: your toolkit. Forget fancy gadgets; you only need a few key tools to cover almost every basic repair in your home or apartment. Here's what you need:

Basic Tools: (The Essentials)

Screwdrivers (Flathead & Phillips): These are the MVPs of any toolkit. Flathead and Phillips (the one with the cross-shaped tip) will handle 90% of the screws you'll encounter. Loose cabinet door? Wonky drawer? These will save the day.

Hammer: A good hammer is crucial. You'll need it for hanging pictures, fixing nails, or putting together IKEA furniture. Tip: opt for a claw hammer so you can pull out nails too.

Pliers (Regular & Needle Nose): These will grip, twist, pull, and hold whatever your fingers can't. Regular pliers are great for grabbing and twisting, while needle-nose pliers can get into smaller, tighter spaces (like fixing jewelry or electrical wires).

Wrench Set: Adjustable wrenches are lifesavers when you're tightening or loosening nuts and bolts. No need for a full set, one or two adjustable wrenches will cover most of your needs.

Tape Measure: You'll never know how often you need one of these until you get one. For hanging pictures, buying furniture, or making sure that new couch will actually fit through your door.

Level: Nothing worse than hanging a shelf or picture, thinking it's perfect, only to realize it's crooked. A small level will make sure everything is lined up perfectly.

Utility Knife: From cutting boxes to trimming carpets or wallpaper, a sharp utility knife is a must-have. Be careful with it though, respect the blade!

Allen Wrenches: If you've ever bought furniture from IKEA, you've probably used one of these. They're those L-shaped wrenches that come with every piece of furniture. Get a set that covers different sizes, and you'll be good to go.

Duct Tape: This stuff is basically magic. You can temporarily fix almost anything with duct tape, from a leaky pipe to a broken chair leg. It's not a permanent solution, but it'll hold things together until you can figure out a better fix.

Upgraded Tools (For When You're Ready to Step Up):

Cordless Drill: Once you've used one of these, you'll never go back. It's great for hanging things, assembling furniture, and tightening screws quickly. Get one with a set of bits, and you're golden.

Stud Finder: If you're hanging something heavy (like a TV mount), you'll want to find a stud (the wood beams behind your walls) to anchor it into. A stud finder helps you avoid drilling into drywall, which isn't strong enough to hold heavy stuff.

Caulking Gun: Got cracks around your windows or bathtub? A caulking gun lets you fill in those gaps to prevent water damage and keep the cold air out.

Plunger: Yes, it's gross, but when your toilet clogs, you'll be glad you have one. Every home needs a plunger, no exceptions.

Fixing the Basics: Essential Home Repair Skills

Mastering these is like having cheat codes for adulthood, you'll skip a lot of frustration and unexpected bills.

Okay, so now you've got your toolkit, but what do you actually *do* with it? Let's break down the most common household issues you'll face and how to fix them, without having to call your dad or Google every step.

Fixing a Leaky Faucet

That constant drip-drip-drip isn't just annoying, it's wasting water and could be driving up your utility bill. The good news is, fixing a leaky faucet is one of the easiest home repairs out there. It's usually a worn-out washer or O-ring that needs replacing. Here's how to do it:

1. **Turn off the water**: This is crucial. There's usually a valve under the sink that cuts the water supply.

2. **Disassemble the faucet**: Use your wrench to unscrew the faucet handle and get to the washer.

3. **Replace the washer**: Most hardware stores sell faucet repair kits that include the washer or O-ring.

4. **Reassemble and test**: Put everything back together, turn the water on, and voila, no more drips.

Unclogging a Sink

Whether it's hair in the bathroom sink or food in the kitchen sink, clogs happen. You don't always need to call a plumber though. Here's what you do:

1. **Try the plunger**: Yep, a plunger works on sinks too. Create a seal and give it a few good pumps to dislodge the clog.

2. **Use a drain snake**: These flexible tools are perfect for pulling out hair and gunk that's clogging your drain. Just be prepared, it's not going to be pretty.

3. **Baking Soda & Vinegar**: For a more eco-friendly option, pour baking soda down the drain, followed by vinegar. It'll bubble up and help clear the blockage.

Fixing a Running Toilet

Is your toilet constantly running? Not only is it annoying, but it's also wasting water. The issue is probably the **flapper**, a rubber piece inside the tank that seals off the water after you flush. Here's how to fix it:

1. **Turn off the water**: Shut off the valve behind the toilet.

2. **Open the tank**: Take off the tank lid and look inside. You'll see a chain attached to the flapper at the bottom.

3. **Replace the flapper**: Pick up a new one from the hardware store (they're cheap). Remove the old one and snap the new one in place.

4. **Test**: Turn the water back on and flush the toilet. No more running.

Patching a Hole in the Wall

Whether you accidentally knocked something into the wall or you're dealing with damage from moving furniture, small holes are easy to fix.

1. **Grab some spackle**: You can find small containers of spackle at any hardware store. Scoop some onto a putty knife and press it into the hole.

2. **Smooth it out**: Scrape off the excess so it's flush with the wall.

3. **Sand it**: Once it dries (usually within an hour), use fine sandpaper to smooth it out.

4. **Paint over it**: If you've got the paint to match your wall, dab a little over the patch, and no one will ever know there was a hole there.

Assembling Furniture Without Throwing It Across the Room

IKEA should sell patience in the same aisle as their Allen wrenches. Until then, stay calm, follow the steps, and keep your snack stash nearby.

Ah, IKEA. The place where dreams of stylish apartments meet the cold reality of furniture assembly. If you've ever felt personally attacked by an IKEA instruction manual, you're not alone. But with a little patience (and some preparation), you can assemble your furniture without losing your mind, or your temper.

The IKEA Survival Guide:

1. **Lay Everything Out**: Before you even think about grabbing a tool, lay out all the pieces and make sure everything is there. Missing a part halfway through is the fastest way to start swearing at a bookshelf.

2. **Read the Instructions**: Yeah, I know. No one likes reading the manual, but with IKEA furniture, you don't have a choice. Follow the steps in order. Skip one, and you'll be disassembling and starting over.

3. **Use Your Own Tools**: Those little Allen wrenches they give you? They work, but a cordless drill with an Allen bit will save you so much time. Just be gentle, over-tightening screws can crack the particle board.

4. **Take Breaks**: If you're feeling frustrated, step away for a minute. Come back with fresh eyes, and it'll make way more sense (I promise).

Bonus Tips: Apartment Hacks Everyone Should Know

Apartment living is just homeownership on training wheels. Learn these hacks, and you'll keep your security deposit and your sanity.

Living in an apartment comes with its own set of challenges, but with a few tricks up your sleeve, you can handle the quirks of rental life without breaking a sweat, or your security deposit.

Wall Mounting Without Damage

Command strips are the duct tape of the rental world, stick 'em, use 'em, and leave without a trace.

Most apartments have strict "no drilling" policies, but you don't need to sacrifice decorating your space. Enter **Command strips and hooks**. These damage-free wonders allow you to hang pictures, shelves, or even hooks for coats and bags without hammering a single nail. Just remember to check the weight limits, so you don't accidentally rip the paint off your wall.

Fixing Squeaky Floors and Doors

Squeaky floors and doors can drive you crazy. Instead of putting up with it (or apologizing to everyone for your ninja moves), here's a quick fix:

> For **squeaky floors**, sprinkle **baby powder** between the boards. It'll help lubricate them and reduce the squeak without having to rip up the floor.

> For **squeaky doors**, apply a little **WD-40** or even cooking oil to the hinges, and swing the door back and forth a few times to work it in. Problem solved, and you've just saved yourself the hassle of calling your landlord.

Drafty Windows? No Problem

If your windows aren't exactly airtight and you're feeling a breeze in the winter, don't freeze, fix it. Grab a window insulation kit from any hardware store (basically plastic sheets and tape) and apply it to the inside of your windows. It keeps the cold air out and helps with your heating bill. Alternatively, using **draft stoppers** along the bottom of your doors or windows can help keep the heat in (or out in summer).

Maximizing Storage in a Tiny Space

Apartments are often notorious for their lack of space, but with some clever thinking, you can maximize what you've got. Try these hacks:

Over-the-Door Organizers: These are perfect for storing shoes, cleaning supplies, or toiletries. Just hang one over a closet or bathroom door to create extra storage.

Under-Bed Storage: Don't let that space under your bed go to waste. Pick up some storage bins and slide them under the bed to store out-of-season clothes, books, or anything else you want out of sight.

Tension Rods: These can be lifesavers in closets or even underneath your kitchen sink to create extra hanging space for cleaning supplies, scarves, or pots and pans.

Temporary Fixes for Rental Wear and Tear

Every apartment starts to show signs of wear and tear, especially when you've lived there a while. You don't want to lose your deposit because of some minor scuffs or scratches, so here are a few **rental-friendly hacks** to keep your place looking sharp:

Magic Erasers: These little cleaning tools can work wonders on scuffed walls, floors, and countertops. Just wet them slightly and gently scrub away the marks.

Touch-Up Paint Pens: If your apartment has painted walls, ask your landlord if they have any leftover paint from the last paint job. You can use a paint pen or small brush to touch up any small chips or scratches, leaving your place looking fresh.

Final Thoughts: From DIY Rookie to Home Maintenance Hero

Mastering basic home maintenance doesn't mean you'll never need help from a pro, but it does mean you'll be able to handle 90% of the stuff that comes up. By knowing how to fix minor issues, manage apartment hacks, and tackle furniture assembly like a champ, you're not just making your life easier, you're also saving money, avoiding panic calls to your landlord, and gaining serious self-sufficiency points.

For the guys, having these skills means you'll never have to feel embarrassed about calling your dad to ask how to unclog a drain. For the girls, wielding a screwdriver or plunger with confidence is just another step toward total independence. By the end of this chapter, you're not just handling the basics, you're owning them. So grab that toolkit, embrace your inner DIY guru, and start fixing stuff like the home repair hero you are.

-- 55 --

Chapter 5: Digital Literacy & Social Media Smarts

In the old days, your reputation was what people saw you do. Now? It's also what you post, like, share, and accidentally tag yourself in at 2 AM.

Welcome to the world where your online presence can either make you look like a social media superstar or... *that person*. We all know them, the oversharer, the serial ghoster, the one who's still arguing in the comment section about pineapple on pizza. In today's digital age, being savvy online isn't just a nice-to-have, it's essential. Whether you're flexing your selfies or just trying to stay connected, let's dive into how to master social media without becoming an internet cautionary tale.

Social Media Etiquette: How to Avoid Being THAT Person

Social media is like a permanent open mic night, fun until you say something you can't take back.

Social media is like a giant cocktail party, fun, full of people, and great for showing off your best self. But here's the catch: just like at any party, there are some unwritten rules to keep things cool.

Ignore them, and congratulations, you've become *that* person everyone rolls their eyes at. Nobody wants that.

1. Think Before You Post (No, Really)

Here's the golden rule of the internet: **if you wouldn't want it on a billboard, don't post it**. That hilarious meme you're thinking of posting? Yeah, maybe not so funny when your future boss (or worse, your grandma) sees it. Social media is forever, folks. Even if you hit delete, you're just one screenshot away from having your questionable choices immortalized. So unless you want your spicy hot take shared at the next family dinner, give it a second thought.

2. Keep Your DMs Classy

Ah, the DM slide, where legends are made or reputations go to die. Newsflash: if you wouldn't say it in person, don't say it online. The number one rule here? **Be respectful**. That means no unsolicited, inappropriate pictures (seriously, do we even need to say this?), no pushing for attention, and definitely no "hey" after being ghosted for the fourth time. Keep it cool, folks. A well-placed joke goes a lot farther than "U up?" at 2 AM.

3. Oversharing: Less is More

We get it, you're excited about your new dog, your lunch, your latest gym session, and that time you saw a rainbow. But does everyone else need to see every single moment of your day? **Probably not**. You don't need to broadcast every meal or gym workout. Sometimes, leaving a little mystery is a good thing. Do you really want to be remembered as the person who posted ten selfies in one day? No, no, you don't.

4. The "No Drama Zone"

You know those people who air every piece of dirty laundry online? Yeah, don't be them. If you've had a fight with your bestie or are low-key mad about your ex's new flame, social media is not your therapy couch. Keep the drama offline, no one needs your passive-aggressive status update. Instead, save it for your group chat or, you know, an actual conversation. You'll thank yourself later.

5. Don't Be a Keyboard Warrior

Sure, it's easy to throw shade or start a debate in the comments, but guess what? **No one wins** in an internet argument. Plus, do you really want to be known as the person who spent three hours fighting over whether "Die Hard" is a Christmas movie? (It is, by the way, but that's beside the point.) Save your energy for real-life battles, or at least ones that involve pizza toppings.

Keeping Your Digital Footprint Clean and Safe

Your online trail is like glitter, once it's out there, it's impossible to clean up completely.

Here's the thing: your digital footprint is like a trail of breadcrumbs you've left all over the internet, and unlike the trails in fairy tales, this one sticks around. Future employers, dates, and friends can all Google you, yep, people are snooping, and what they find could haunt you.

1. Google Yourself (No Shame)

The easiest way to see what's out there? **Google yourself**. No, it's not narcissistic; it's smart. See what comes up and check if there's anything cringe-worthy (like that Twitter rant from high school or your awkward prom pictures). If you don't like what you see, now's the time to clean it up. Untag yourself, delete, or hide the stuff you wouldn't want to explain during a job interview.

2. Mind Your Privacy Settings

You wouldn't leave your front door wide open, would you? Treat your social media accounts the same way. Take a few minutes to dive into your privacy settings and make sure you're only sharing your personal life with the people you trust. That means no posting everything publicly, unless you want random strangers knowing about your weekend plans.

3. Avoid Sketchy Websites and Clickbait

We've all been tempted by clickbait: "You Won't Believe What This Celebrity Looks Like Now!" But here's the truth: **don't click it**. Sketchy websites are prime territory for malware, and you don't want your laptop (or your phone) infected because you needed to see which Kardashian changed their hair color. Stick to reputable sites, and if something seems too good to be true, it probably is.

4. Stay Off Public Wi-Fi for Important Stuff

We all love free Wi-Fi, but public networks are a hacker's playground. Avoid logging into your bank, shopping online, or anything sensitive while connected to Starbucks' free Wi-Fi. Save the important stuff for when you're home and on a secured connection. Unless, of course, you want to explain why someone else bought $500 worth of cat sweaters with your credit card.

How to Balance Screen Time Without FOMO

Your phone is a tool, not a life support machine. Don't let it run the show.

Let's be real, social media can be addictive. Between Instagram stories, Snapchat streaks, and TikTok rabbit holes, it's easy to spend hours scrolling through other people's lives and wondering if you're missing out on something. But the key to keeping your sanity and avoiding full-blown burnout is finding a balance.

1. The 1:1 Rule

Here's a trick for you: for every hour you spend online, spend one hour doing something offline. Whether it's going for a walk, hanging out with friends IRL, or reading a book (*yes, books still exist*), it'll help you break the cycle of endless scrolling. Plus, it makes your online time feel more like a reward rather than a mindless habit.

2. Social Media Sabbaticals Are Legit

Sometimes, you just need a break. Social media can make you feel like you're always missing out, but guess what? The world keeps turning whether you're watching stories or not. Taking a day or even a weekend off from social media can do wonders for your mental health. Plus, when you come back, your feed will still be there waiting for you, and now you won't have to deal with the envy-inducing beach pics while you're stuck at work.

3. Set Limits (Literally)

Most smartphones have built-in screen time trackers. Use them. Set limits for how long you want to spend on apps like Instagram, Snapchat, or TikTok. When you hit your limit, the app will nudge you to take a break. And let's be honest, if you've been on TikTok for two hours straight, a break is *definitely* in order.

4. Real Life is Happening Right Now

Here's the thing: social media only shows the highlights. It's the best parts of people's lives, not the full picture. So while you're sitting at home in sweatpants, remember that the person posting about their amazing vacation also has bad days, they just don't post about them. Don't compare your behind-the-scenes to everyone else's highlight reel. The real world is happening right now, and you don't want to miss it because you're too busy watching someone else's story.

Final Thoughts: Own Your Digital Life

The internet can make you or break you. Use it like a spotlight, shine it where you want the world to look.

Mastering the art of digital literacy isn't just about knowing how to post a cute selfie (although that's a skill too). It's about navigating the online world with confidence, class, and a touch of caution. Social media is a powerful tool, use it wisely, and it can help you connect, create, and have fun. But misuse it, and it can turn into a minefield of cringe-worthy mistakes and headaches.

For the guys, knowing your way around digital etiquette will save you from embarrassing DMs and keep you from being "that guy." For the girls, staying on top of your digital footprint will ensure you keep your social media game strong without sacrificing your personal brand. At the end of the day, it's all about balance, use social media to enhance your life, not control it.

-- 63 --

Adulting 101: Life Skills for Growing Up

Chapter 6: Entrepreneurial Skills

From Side Hustle to CEO

So, you've got big dreams of being the next Steve Jobs or maybe you just want to make some extra cash without selling your soul to a 9-to-5. Either way, the entrepreneurial path calls to those who hate the idea of someone else telling them when they can take lunch. Whether you're looking to build a personal brand that slaps, network your way to success, or start a side hustle that might just take over your life, I'm here to walk you through the madness. The goal? To help you go from dabbling in side gigs to maybe, just maybe, running your own empire.

Building Your Personal Brand Before You Hit 25

Alright, let's get something straight right off the bat: your **personal brand** isn't just for influencers trying to sell you detox tea on Instagram. Nope, it's for anyone who's serious about making a mark on the world. Whether you're starting your own business, creating content, or just figuring out your career, your personal brand is your calling card, and the sooner you start building it, the better.

1. What Is a Personal Brand, Anyway?

Think of your personal brand as the way people describe you when you're not in the room. Do they say, "Oh, yeah, she's the girl who's really into sustainability," or "He's that guy who can turn anything into a profitable side hustle"? It's about who you are, what you stand for, and what you want people to remember about you.

Uncle Aaron's Take: *If you're out here posting memes one minute and LinkedIn think pieces the next, your brand is gonna feel like a confused emoji. Stay consistent. Think about your strengths, what you're passionate about, and start building your image around that. You don't have to know all the answers, just have a general direction. Plus, it's way easier to be authentic when you're not faking it.*

2. Start Building Your Brand Right Now

Here's the good news: you don't need to have your life completely figured out to start building a personal brand. But here's the catch, every post, every comment, every move you make online is shaping that brand. So, think twice before you post that questionable meme or go on a public rant about how much you hate Mondays. No one wants to hire the guy who's always complaining on Twitter, and trust me, your future clients will stalk your Instagram.

Practical Steps:

Clean Up Your Socials: I'm not saying you need to delete every party pic, but do you really want potential business partners seeing you passed out at Coachella? Keep it fun but keep it professional.

Find Your Niche: What do you want to be known for? Whether it's creating killer websites, designing streetwear, or making candles that smell like success, get specific. People don't remember vague; they remember unique.

Be Consistent: Make sure your message is the same across platforms. Your Instagram bio, LinkedIn, and website should all point to the same brand. You don't want to come off as a different person on each platform, it's confusing and nobody trusts that.

3. Make Connections Early

Your brand doesn't exist in a vacuum. The people you connect with will help shape how others see you, and let's be real, networking is half the game. If you want to build a brand that's recognizable, make sure you're connected with people who are doing the kinds of things you aspire to do.

Networking for Success: The Right Way to Make Connections

Here's the truth: networking isn't just for sleazy salespeople or that one friend who's "into crypto." It's one of the most powerful tools you have, and the best part? You don't need a business degree or a fancy suit to do it. Networking is just about building genuine relationships, and if you do it right, it doesn't even have to feel like networking.

1. Get Over the Awkwardness

Networking sounds like this big, scary thing where you awkwardly shake hands and swap business cards, right? Wrong. Networking is just talking to people and making connections that benefit both of you. It's not about what you can take, it's about building relationships that last.

Tip: *Everyone's a little awkward. The trick is not to care. Treat networking like a conversation, not a business transaction. Ask questions, listen, and find common ground. People love talking about themselves, so let them!*

2. Where to Network

There are tons of places to network, and it's not just boring conferences or LinkedIn. Here's where you should start:

Social media: Twitter, Instagram, and LinkedIn are gold mines for meeting people in your industry. Follow people who are doing what you want to do and engage with their content. It's way less creepy than you think. Just be genuine.

Events & Meetups: If you're serious about your hustle, start showing up to industry events, meetups, and even virtual workshops. Bring your A-game, have a few conversation starters, and remember you're there to build relationships, not just pitch yourself.

Friend of a Friend: Never underestimate your existing network. If you've got friends who know people in the industry you're interested in, don't be shy, ask for introductions. Most people are happy to help connect the dots.

3. Play the Long Game

Networking isn't about immediate returns; it's about planting seeds. Maybe you connect with someone today, but they don't have an opportunity for you yet. That's fine. Keep in touch, engage with their work, and who knows? In six months or a year, you might be top of mind when something pops up.

Starting a Side Hustle: How to Make Cash and Still Have Fun

Look, not everyone's cut out to jump straight into full-time entrepreneurship, and that's fine. But almost everyone can benefit from a good old-fashioned **side hustle**. Whether you're looking to make some extra cash or test the waters before diving headfirst into business ownership, a side hustle is where the magic happens.

1. The Side Hustle Sweet Spot

First things first: pick something you enjoy. The whole point of a side hustle is that it doesn't feel like a soul-sucking second job. Find something you're good at, passionate about, and something people will actually pay for.

Need ideas? Here are a few that might inspire you:

Freelancing: If you've got skills, writing, graphic design, social media management, turn them into cash. Sites like Upwork, Fiverr, and even LinkedIn can help you get started.

Sell a Product: Got a knack for making cool stuff? Whether it's homemade candles, jewelry, or even art, Etsy is the place for creators to sell their wares. You might start small, but trust me, it can snowball.

Content Creation: If you've got a personality and a passion for something (like fitness, fashion, gaming), why not create content around it? Between YouTube, TikTok, and Instagram, creators are making bank just by being themselves.

The goal? Make money while doing something that doesn't suck your soul out through your eyeballs.

2. Side Hustles Aren't a Free Pass to Slack

Let's be clear: just because it's a side hustle doesn't mean you can half-ass it. Treat your hustle like a business, even if it's just part-time for now. That means staying organized, setting deadlines, and delivering quality work. Nothing kills a side hustle faster than laziness.

Tip: *Your side hustle might not be your dream job, but it's your **ticket** to freedom. Think of it as your launchpad. Today, you're freelancing for a few bucks, but who knows? Tomorrow, you could be running your own show.*

3. Balancing Fun and Business

Here's where a lot of side hustlers crash and burn: they forget that balance is key. You still have a life, friends, family, and probably another job or school to handle. Don't let your hustle take over completely. Set boundaries, take breaks, and make sure you're still having fun.

Running a side hustle is like juggling: if you try to keep too many things in the air, something's going to fall. Pace yourself, focus on growing your business *and* your life, and remember, you're the boss of your hustle, not the other way around.

Final Thoughts: From Side Hustler to CEO

So, you've got the tools to build your personal brand, network like a pro, and launch a side hustle. What's next? Keep grinding, keep learning, and don't be afraid to take the leap when the time comes. You might start small, but everyone does. The secret to success is simple: consistency, passion, and the ability to laugh when things get crazy.

Boys, being your own boss isn't just about flexing, it's about freedom. Girls, breaking into the entrepreneurial game means having control over your career and your future. Whoever you are, whatever you're hustling for, just know that you can make it happen. You've got the skills, the drive, and (hopefully) a great playlist to keep you motivated.

Now go out there and start building something awesome.

Chapter 7: Communication and Emotional Intelligence

Here's a secret no one talks about enough: in a world full of texts, tweets, and TikToks, *actually talking* to people face-to-face still matters, *a lot*. Yeah, I know, it's tempting to live behind your screen where you can carefully craft responses and add the perfect emoji for effect, but in real life, you don't have that luxury. Communication isn't just about talking; it's about listening, connecting, and knowing when to stop before things get awkward.

On top of that, we've got **emotional intelligence** to deal with. Before you roll your eyes and swipe to the next chapter, hear me out, understanding your emotions and how to read other people's is your cheat code to life. Trust me, whether you're at work, in a relationship, or trying to navigate group projects, emotional intelligence will help you keep your cool and not blow up when someone says something stupid.

Oh, and let's not forget the biggest challenge of all: **disagreeing without turning it into a full-blown flame war**. Spoiler alert: it's possible to disagree without throwing verbal punches (or real ones), and I'm here to show you how. Let's dive in.

Mastering Face-to-Face Communication
(Yes, It Still Matters)

Okay, let's talk about real-world communication, the kind where you're staring at an actual human being and not typing away behind a screen. I know, it sounds terrifying, but here's the thing: mastering face-to-face communication is like having a superpower in a world where everyone's glued to their phones. Whether it's a job interview, meeting someone new, or just making a good impression, knowing how to *talk* is critical.

1. Eye Contact: Not a Staring Contest, but Close

Look, I'm not saying you need to lock eyes with someone like you're in a weird staring contest, but eye contact is key. It shows you're paying attention and not just thinking about what you're going to say next. If you're constantly looking away, it makes you seem distracted or disinterested, both of which are bad looks.

But here's the trick: don't overdo it. Too much eye contact can make things uncomfortable real fast. The sweet spot? Look at the person when they're talking to you, nod every now and then, and glance away occasionally to avoid creeping them out.

2. Body Language: Speak Without Saying a Word

Did you know most communication is non-verbal? That means your body is saying things even when your mouth isn't. Crossing your arms? You look defensive. Slouching? You look like you'd rather be anywhere else. The key here is to keep your body language open and approachable.

- **Stand or sit up straight**: It makes you look confident.

- **Uncross your arms**: It signals you're open to the conversation.

- **Use gestures**: Not like you're trying to conduct an orchestra, but enough to show you're engaged.

And guys, don't fidget like you've got ants in your pants. It's distracting. Girls, same goes for twirling your hair or constantly adjusting your clothes, stay calm and collected.

3. Active Listening: It's More Than Just Nodding

Here's the thing: listening isn't just about waiting for your turn to talk. It's about actually *hearing* what the other person is saying. Active listening involves nodding (appropriately), giving verbal cues like "Yeah" or "I see," and asking follow-up questions. It shows you're paying attention and not just mentally checking out.

Tip: *Repeat back what the person said in your own words. It confirms that you understood, and it helps keep the conversation flowing. Plus, people love it when they feel heard, trust me, it works like magic.*

4. Know When to Stop Talking

This one's for both the over-sharers and the awkward silencers: conversations are a two-way street. If you're dominating the conversation, the other person is going to mentally check out. On the flip side, if you're not contributing at all, they'll think you're not interested. Find the balance.

Here's the rule: share something, ask a question, listen to the answer, repeat. Don't hog the spotlight, but don't fade into the background either. If you can master this, you'll be a conversational legend in no time.

Emotional Intelligence: How to Keep Your Cool (and Understand Others)

You've probably heard the term **emotional intelligence** thrown around before, but let's break it down: emotional intelligence (EQ) is your ability to recognize, understand, and manage your own emotions, while also being aware of the emotions of others. In other words, it's about being the chill one in stressful situations and knowing when someone's on the verge of losing it.

1. Recognize Your Own Emotions

The first step to mastering emotional intelligence is knowing what's going on inside your own head. Are you mad? Frustrated? Sad? Hangry? (Yes, that's a real emotion). The faster you can identify what you're feeling, the faster you can control it.

Here's where people get tripped up: emotions don't just "happen" to you. You have the power to take a step back and decide how to respond. Feel a rant coming on? Pause. Ready to lose it in traffic? Breathe. Recognizing that you're about to go off the rails gives you a chance to steer the train back onto the tracks.

2. Manage Your Reactions

Ever had someone say something dumb, and you're about two seconds away from launching into a full-blown rant? Yeah, we've all been there. But here's the thing: how you react is everything.

Instead of immediately firing back, take a beat. Give yourself a second to process what they said and decide if it's worth the energy. More often than not, it's not. Save yourself the headache and keep your cool. The more you practice this, the better you'll get at controlling your emotions, like a zen master who also happens to have Wi-Fi.

3. Empathy: The Secret Sauce to Social Superpowers

Empathy is your ability to put yourself in someone else's shoes. It's about recognizing what the other person is feeling and responding accordingly. And no, it's not about being a doormat or agreeing with everyone, but understanding where they're coming from can help you communicate more effectively.

Here's how to level up your empathy game:

- **Listen to understand, not just to respond**.

- **Acknowledge their emotions**: Even if you don't agree with their point, saying, "I get that this is frustrating for you," can diffuse a lot of tension.

- **Ask questions**: Instead of assuming you know how they feel, ask. You'd be surprised how much people appreciate someone actually taking an interest.

4. The Power of a Pause

When things are getting heated, it's easy to let your emotions get the best of you. But one of the most powerful tools in your emotional intelligence toolkit is the **pause**. Before reacting, take a breath, count to five (or ten, if necessary), and then respond. That tiny moment of pause can stop you from saying something you'll regret later.

How to Disagree Without Turning It Into a Flame War

Ah, the art of disagreement. Whether it's over politics, pineapple on pizza, or whether cats are better than dogs (they're not, fight me), knowing how to disagree without throwing verbal punches is a skill we all need. The good news? It's totally possible to disagree without escalating things into a full-blown flame war. And the best part is, it can be done with class, humor, and maybe even a little charm. Here's how.

1. Stay Calm, Cool, and Collected

First things first: **don't lose your cool**. When you're in the middle of a disagreement, it's easy to let your emotions take over. You start feeling heated, your pulse quickens, and before you know it, you're either yelling or typing in **ALL CAPS**, which, let's face it, never helps anyone win an argument. Once things get emotional, the conversation has already taken a turn for the worse.

So how do you stay calm? **Keep your voice steady** and your tone neutral. Breathe before you speak or type. If you feel yourself getting agitated, take a step back, give it a minute, and then respond. Remember, the goal isn't to "win" by overpowering the other person, it's to get your point across and maybe (just maybe) make them see where you're coming from.

Tip: *If you're arguing in real life and not on a keyboard, keep your body language in check. No aggressive postures or wild hand gestures, no one responds well to that.*

2. Listen (For Real) Before Responding

Here's the thing most people forget during a disagreement: **listening is half the battle**. When someone is presenting their side, stop thinking about what you're going to say next, and actually hear them out. If you don't listen, you're not going to get anywhere. Listening shows that you respect the other person's opinion, even if it's way off-base in your mind (like pineapple on pizza, seriously).

Active listening means you're nodding, giving feedback like, "I see what you're saying," or "That's an interesting point." This doesn't mean you're agreeing with them, but it signals that you're engaged in the conversation. Once you've fully heard them out, *then* it's your turn to speak.

Bonus Tip: *Paraphrase what they said before you respond. It shows you understand their argument, and then you can calmly dismantle it (with love, of course).*

3. Don't Make It Personal

Rule number one of avoiding a flame war: **don't make it personal**. As soon as you start attacking someone's character instead of their argument, things are going to go south fast. Stick to the topic at hand, and avoid phrases like "you always" or "you never." These types of sweeping generalizations will only escalate the situation.

For example, if you're debating the merits of pineapple on pizza, don't say, "You're insane if you like pineapple on pizza," instead, go with something like, "I get that you like pineapple, but for me, the sweetness throws off the balance." See? Way more civilized and less likely to start a digital fistfight.

Tip: *Don't be passive-aggressive. It's tempting, but it'll just make the other person defensive, and no one wins when that happens.*

4. Find Common Ground

Even in the heat of disagreement, there's often **common ground** to be found. Maybe you both agree that pizza is amazing, even if you differ on toppings. Maybe you both care about the same issues, but your solutions are different. Finding that common ground can help de-escalate the tension and bring the conversation back to a more productive place.

When you're able to say, "I agree with you on that, but I see it differently when it comes to this part," it helps to shift the conversation into a more constructive space. You're no longer just opponents, you're people who share at least one view, and that makes disagreement a little easier to handle.

Example: *"Look, we both agree pizza is the best food on earth. I'm just saying, pineapple doesn't belong anywhere near it."*

5. Choose Your Battles

Not every disagreement is worth having, and sometimes, the smartest thing you can do is just let it go. If you realize halfway through that the argument isn't actually important, or that it's going nowhere, **bow out gracefully**. There's no shame in saying, "You know what? We're not going to agree on this, and that's okay. Let's agree to disagree."

Choosing your battles means knowing when to push and when to back off. Some hills just aren't worth dying on, especially when it comes to things like social media arguments that spiral out of control. Ask yourself: "Is this argument actually worth it?" Nine times out of ten, the answer is probably "no."

6. Use Humor to Diffuse the Situation

Humor can be a **powerful weapon** in any disagreement, as long as it's used wisely. A well-placed joke or light-hearted comment can take the edge off and remind everyone that you're all human, even if you disagree. The key is to keep the humor respectful and not make it a dig at the other person.

For example, if the conversation is getting a little heated, you can throw in something like, "Okay, let's just agree that pineapple is divisive and that pizza is awesome no matter what's on it." It lightens the mood and reminds the other person that, at the end of the day, you're not mortal enemies, you're just two people who have different tastes in pizza.

Tip: *Avoid sarcasm, especially online. It's way too easy for sarcasm to be misinterpreted as an insult, and that's the last thing you want.*

Final Thoughts: Disagree Like a Pro

Disagreeing doesn't have to mean going to war. Whether it's an argument about politics, food, or something a little deeper, knowing how to navigate the conversation without losing your cool is a skill that'll serve you for life. Stay calm, listen, find common ground, and don't be afraid to use a little humor. After all, if we all agreed on everything, life would be pretty boring.

So the next time someone says something that makes your blood boil, just remember it's possible to disagree without turning it into a drama-filled showdown. And who knows? You might even learn something along the way.

-- 82 --

Chapter 8: Health, Wellness, and the Mind-Body Connection

Alright, listen up. Health and wellness aren't about spending all your time sweating it out at a fancy gym or living off kale smoothies. Nope. Uncle Aaron's got a better way for you, one that involves keeping your mind sharp, your body moving, and your bank account intact. You don't need to be a fitness junkie or a meditation guru to stay healthy. You just need to balance things out and take care of yourself without going overboard. So, let's jump into how you can crush this whole "wellness" thing like a pro without losing your mind, or your pizza.

The Basics of Staying Fit Without a Gym Membership

Let me drop a truth bomb right here: **you do not need a gym** to get in shape. In fact, you don't need fancy machines, protein shakes, or one of those trainers who yells motivational slogans while you cry. All you need is a little space, your body, and maybe the willpower to get off the couch (I know, easier said than done, but stick with me).

1. Bodyweight Exercises: Your Free Fitness Plan

Your body is already a workout machine. Yep, it's got everything you need to stay in shape, and the best part? It's 100% portable. We're talking **push-ups**, **squats**, **planks**, **lunges**, all those classic moves you've probably seen people do at the park and thought, "That looks easy." Spoiler: it's not. But it works. These exercises hit all the right muscles and can be done anywhere: living room, backyard, even during TV commercials.

Tip: *Start small. No need to go full Rocky Balboa on day one. Try doing 10 push-ups, 15 squats, and holding a plank for 30 seconds. Then, when you're not sore to the point of questioning your life choices, gradually increase the reps. And remember, breaks are your friend, embrace them.*

2. Walking: The Unsung Hero of Workouts

You know those people who think they need to run marathons to stay fit? Bless their hearts. Meanwhile, **walking**, yep, just plain walking, is the sneaky underdog of the fitness world. You burn calories, get some fresh air, and avoid the feeling that your lungs are about to explode. Walk your dog, walk to the store, walk while listening to a podcast, just walk.

Tip: *Take it up a notch by finding some hills or walking at a brisk pace (basically just speed up like you're in a hurry to grab the last slice of pizza). Walking is so chill that you won't even realize you're working out until you're ready to collapse.*

3. YouTube Workouts: Your Free Personal Trainer

Can't make it to the gym? Not interested in paying someone to yell at you for slacking on burpees? Welcome to the wonderful world of **YouTube workouts**. The beauty of YouTube is that it's got everything: yoga, HIIT, dance, bodyweight training, whatever gets you moving. Plus, you can do it all from the comfort of your living room in your pajamas. No judgment.

Tip: *Start with beginner videos. Nothing too extreme, just enough to break a sweat. And the best part? You don't have to hear anyone grunting in the background, unless it's your own. Search for "beginner HIIT" or "15-minute full-body workout" and boom, you're good to go.*

Mind-Body Wellness: Yoga, Meditation, and Mental Health

Now that we've got the physical part down, let's talk about the mind. If your brain is a mess, your body will follow. So, whether you're stressed out, overwhelmed, or just need a break from everything, here's how to get your head in the game, without becoming that person who talks about their "third eye" at parties.

1. Yoga: Flexibility for the Soul (and Muscles)

Okay, so yoga might sound like it's all about bending in weird ways, but it's actually one of the best ways to keep both your body and mind in check. Plus, it's great for stretching out those muscles after a hard workout, or a hard day of doing absolutely nothing. You don't have to twist yourself into a pretzel to get the benefits. Yoga helps with flexibility, strength, and calming that stress we all carry around.

Tip: *Don't worry about being perfect or looking like those Instagram yogis. You do you. Start with the basics, like downward dog or child's pose, and slowly build from there. And hey, if all else fails, at least you've got an excuse to lie down for a few minutes.*

2. Meditation: Because Life is Chaotic

Meditation is like a mental vacation you can take anywhere, except without the overpriced tickets and airport security checks. Whether you're stressing out over school, work, or just trying to find peace in the chaos of life, **meditation** helps you stay grounded. And the best part? It's free and requires absolutely zero athletic ability. It's basically the opposite of CrossFit.

Tip: *Start small. Don't try to meditate for an hour like some kind of spiritual warrior. Two or five minutes a day is enough to get you started. Just sit somewhere quiet, close your eyes, and focus on your breathing. That's it. Apps like **Headspace** or **Calm** can guide you, but honestly, just zoning out for a few minutes works wonders too.*

3. Mental Health: It's Not Optional

Here's a truth bomb: your **mental health** is just as important as your physical health. That means making time to unwind, de-stress, and take care of that space between your ears. Whether it's journaling, talking to friends, or scheduling a weekly gaming session to blow off steam, you need to make mental self-care a priority.

Tip: *If things start to feel overwhelming, don't hesitate to talk to someone, whether it's a friend, family member, or a therapist. Keeping your mental health in check isn't a sign of weakness; it's a sign that you're smart enough to take care of yourself.*

Food as Fuel: Eating Well Without Going Broke

Alright, time to talk about **food**. Spoiler alert: food is not your enemy, and you don't have to starve yourself to stay healthy. In fact, food is your body's fuel, so it's all about what kind of gas you're putting in the tank. And no, you don't have to sell your soul (or your budget) to eat well. Let's talk smart, budget-friendly eating.

1. Eating Healthy Without Breaking the Bank

Healthy eating has a bad rep for being expensive, but that's just a myth created by overpriced grocery stores and avocado addicts. You can eat healthy without draining your wallet, you just have to shop smart. Stick to **whole foods** like rice, beans, veggies, and lean meats. These basics are cheap, filling, and good for you.

Tip: *Make a grocery list and stick to it. And don't fall for the "organic everything" trap. Regular carrots will do just fine. Also, buy in bulk when you can, it saves money and keeps you stocked up on essentials like oats, pasta, and grains.*

2. Meal Prep Like a Boss

You want to know the secret to eating healthy on a budget? **Meal prep**. That's right, prepping your meals ahead of time not only saves you money, but also saves you from the temptation of ordering pizza when you're too lazy to cook. And let's be real, we've all been there. Spend one day a week making big batches of food you can eat throughout the week, easy peasy.

Tip: *Start with simple stuff like roasted chicken, rice, and veggies. Mix and match to keep things interesting, and boom, you've got meals for days.*

Also, get some decent food containers because there's nothing worse than your prepped lunch leaking all over your bag.

3. Real Food vs. Junk Food: The Battle Rages On

Let's be honest: **junk food** is delicious, but if you live off chips and soda, your body's going to start feeling like a garbage dump. Don't get me wrong, there's nothing wrong with indulging every now and then, but most of the time, stick to real food that fuels your body and keeps you going strong. Think lean proteins, fruits, veggies, and whole grains.

Tip: *When you do treat yourself, enjoy it. No guilt. Just balance it out with the good stuff so you don't feel like a human Dorito. Everything in moderation, folks. Life's too short to give up burgers forever.*

Final Thoughts: Uncle Aaron's Wellness Wisdom

At the end of the day, **health and wellness** aren't about extremes. It's not about going all-in on one fitness trend or starving yourself to reach some unrealistic goal. It's about balance. Taking care of your body with exercise (even if it's just a walk), keeping your mind sharp with meditation (or just a little quiet time), and eating food that fuels you (without going bankrupt).

Guys, don't think this whole wellness thing is just for the ladies. Taking care of your body and mind is something every smart guy should be doing. **Girls**, don't feel like you need to follow every diet or wellness trend out there

-- 91 --

TAKE A
STEP BACK
BREAK IT
DOWN
BE REALISTIC
ABOUT
SOLUTIONS

Chapter 9: Critical Thinking and Problem Solving

Alright, let's talk about something that can make you a total life ninja: **critical thinking**. We live in a world full of noise, social media, 24-hour news cycles, and endless clickbait. Everyone's trying to get your attention, but if you're not careful, you'll end up believing that the earth is flat or that one weird trick can magically make you rich. Spoiler: it won't. Critical thinking and problem-solving are how you cut through the BS and make smart decisions without losing your cool.

How to Approach Life's Problems Without Freaking Out

Here's the thing: life's problems can feel overwhelming, like when your phone's at 1% and there's no charger in sight. But unlike your phone battery, freaking out won't fix the problem. Learning how to approach issues calmly and methodically is key to avoiding full-blown meltdowns. Whether it's a small issue like a misplaced wallet or something bigger, like deciding what to do with your life (no pressure), you need a strategy.

1. Take a Step Back

When something goes wrong, your first instinct might be to panic (thanks, brain!). But let me tell you, panicking helps no one. The first thing you need to do is **take a step back**. Literally. Remove yourself from the problem for a second and give your brain some breathing room. Walk away, take a deep breath, maybe throw on some music. Once you've calmed down, you can start looking at the issue more rationally.

2. Break It Down

Big problems are scary because they feel like a giant puzzle with a thousand pieces. The trick? **Break it down** into smaller, bite-sized pieces. Don't focus on the whole mountain; focus on climbing one step at a time. If you've got a problem that seems massive, ask yourself: "What's the first thing I can do to start fixing this?" Then, tackle that.

Tip: *Life problems are like Ikea furniture. They seem impossible at first, but if you take it step-by-step, follow the instructions (okay, maybe not those), and resist the urge to throw a wrench through the wall, you'll get through it.*

3. Be Realistic About Solutions

Sometimes, you won't be able to fix everything at once, and that's okay. Be **realistic** about what you can control and what you can't. Not every problem has a perfect solution, and that's life. Focus on doing the best you can with what you've got and be okay with things not being 100% perfect.

Critical Thinking in a World Full of Clickbait

In today's world, you've got clickbait headlines screaming at you, YouTube algorithms trying to suck you into conspiracy theories, and everyone with a Wi-Fi connection claiming to be an expert. So how do you navigate all this noise? With **critical thinking**, that's how.

1. Ask Questions, Lots of Them

The number one rule of critical thinking is to **question everything**. Don't just take things at face value, especially when they're delivered with flashy headlines like "This One Trick Will Change Your Life Forever!" Spoiler: it won't. Start asking yourself questions like, "Who's saying this?" "Why are they saying it?" and "What evidence do they have to back this up?"

Tip: *If it sounds too good to be true, it probably is. Trust me, if someone really had a way to make you a millionaire overnight, they wouldn't be selling it for $19.99 in an eBook.*

2. Check Your Sources

Not all information is created equal. Just because someone posts a video on TikTok doesn't mean it's based on facts (shocking, I know). Before you believe or share something, **check your sources**. Is the information coming from a credible place? Are there experts backing it up? If it's just someone ranting into their camera about the latest "scandal," maybe do a quick fact-check before you retweet.

3. Don't Fall for Confirmation Bias

We're all guilty of it, only paying attention to the stuff that confirms what we already believe and ignoring the rest. But **confirmation bias** is the enemy of critical thinking. If you're only looking for info that backs up your own opinions, you're not learning; you're just reinforcing your bubble. Step outside your comfort zone, read opposing views, and stay open to changing your mind when the facts say you should.

Simple Decision-Making Hacks for Everyday Life

You make decisions every day, whether it's deciding what to eat for dinner or figuring out which career path to take. Some decisions are small, some are huge, but they all require a bit of thought. Here are some **decision-making hacks** that will save you time, energy, and mental breakdowns.

1. Use the Two-Minute Rule

For small decisions, the **two-minute rule** is your new best friend. If a decision will take less than two minutes to make, just make it and move on. Don't waste time agonizing over whether to wear the blue or black shirt, just pick one and get on with your day.

2. The Pros and Cons List: Classic for a Reason

When you're faced with a bigger decision, it's easy to get caught up in the what-ifs. That's where the **pros and cons list** comes in. Yes, it's basic, but it works. Write down all the positives and negatives of each option, then weigh them up. It helps you get everything out of your head and onto paper, so you can see the decision more clearly.

Tip: *Make sure you're being honest with yourself when you're writing those pros and cons. Don't just list a bunch of "pros" for the thing you already want to do. Be real with yourself, or what's the point?*

3. Ask Yourself, "What's the Worst That Could Happen?"

This might sound like bad advice, but it's actually golden. If you're stuck making a decision, sometimes it helps to ask yourself, "What's the worst that could happen?" Once you realize the worst-case scenario isn't that bad, it takes a lot of the pressure off. Most decisions won't ruin your life, so stop treating them like they will.

4. Flip a Coin, Seriously

Stuck between two options? **Flip a coin**. I know it sounds ridiculous but hear me out. When the coin is in the air, you'll instantly know which option you're hoping it lands on. It's not about leaving your fate to chance, it's about tapping into your gut instinct.

Final Thoughts: Thinking Like a Pro

At the end of the day, **critical thinking and problem-solving** are about staying calm, asking the right questions, and using your brain to navigate life's challenges. Whether it's filtering through clickbait headlines or figuring out what to do with your life, approaching things with a level head will get you far.

Guys, don't just rush into decisions because it's easy. And **girls**, trust your instincts, but don't let your emotions cloud your judgment. Whoever you are, remember that life's problems are just puzzles waiting to be solved, one step at a time.

Chapter 10: Stress Management

Chilling Out Without Checking Out

Alright, let's talk about **stress**, the thing that sneaks up on you when you're juggling a million things or just trying to decide whether to cook or order takeout (let's be real, probably takeout). Stress is everywhere, but freaking out won't make it disappear. The trick is learning how to manage it before it turns you into a walking stress ball. Luckily, Uncle Aaron's here to show you how to chill out, without checking out.

Recognizing When You're Stressed
(Hint: It's Sooner Than You Think)

The problem with stress is that it's sneaky. It doesn't always show up with a neon sign saying, "Hey, you're stressed!" Sometimes it's more subtle, like when you've had five cups of coffee but still feel exhausted, or you've responded to every text with "k" because full sentences are just too much right now.

1. The Physical Signs

Your body's like a car with warning lights, if you pay attention, it'll tell you when it's time for maintenance. Headaches, tight shoulders, random jaw clenching? All signs that you might be more stressed than you think. When your body starts acting up, it's usually a signal that stress is hanging out in the background, even if you're too busy to notice.

Tip: *Check in with yourself regularly. Feeling irritable for no reason? That's a red flag. Are you tired but wired? Another clue. The earlier you catch these signs, the easier it is to manage your stress before it manages you.*

2. Emotional Roller Coasters

If your emotions are all over the place, one minute you're laughing at a meme, the next you're rage-texting because someone cut you off in traffic, you might be dealing with stress. Stress doesn't just make you tired; it messes with your mood, too.

Tip: *Watch how you react to small stuff. If minor annoyances are turning into full-blown frustrations, it's time to hit pause and figure out where all that stress is coming from.*

Quick Stress Relief Techniques for Busy Lives

We all know life gets hectic. Between work, social obligations, and trying to binge the latest Netflix show, finding time to chill seems impossible. But stress relief doesn't have to mean booking a weekend retreat to the mountains (although that'd be nice). Here are some quick, effective ways to get your zen on, without needing to rearrange your entire life.

1. The 5-Minute Reset

You've got five minutes, right? That's all you need for a quick mental reset. Whether you're at work or home, step away from whatever's stressing you out and **breathe**. Yeah, it sounds too simple, but a few minutes of deep breathing works wonders for calming your mind and slowing down that racing heart.

Tip: *Close your eyes, take slow breaths, and count to four as you inhale, hold for four, then exhale for four. Rinse and repeat until you feel your shoulders drop from up around your ears.*

2. Move Your Body (No Gym Required)

When stress hits, your body gets tense. You don't need to hit the gym for a full workout, just **move**. Stretch, take a walk, or if you're feeling fancy, do a few jumping jacks. Movement releases endorphins, which are basically nature's stress antidote.

Tip: *Have a little mini-dance party. Put on your favorite song and just let loose for a minute. I guarantee you'll feel less stressed by the time the chorus hits.*

3. The Magic of Laughing at Stupid Things

Laughter really is the best medicine. When stress has you feeling like a bundle of nerves, take five minutes to watch something funny. Memes, cat videos, stand-up comedy, whatever gets you giggling. It's scientifically proven to lower stress hormones, and let's be real, it's way more fun than crying into your pillow.

Tip: *Keep a list of go-to funny content. That way, when you're feeling the stress creep up, you've got instant access to something that'll make you laugh and forget about your worries for a bit.*

Work-Life Balance: Yes, It's Possible

I know what you're thinking: "Work-life balance? That's a myth, right?" Not exactly. It *is* possible to balance your job, school, hobbies, friends, and everything else life throws at you, without feeling like you're constantly sprinting from one thing to the next. But, it does take some effort to set boundaries and keep your stress in check.

1. Set Clear Boundaries

When you're working or studying from home, it's easy to let the lines between work and personal life blur. Suddenly, you're answering emails at 9 PM or stressing about school assignments during dinner. The trick is to **set boundaries**. Create clear "work time" and "you time," and stick to them.

Tip: *At the end of your work or study day, physically step away from your workspace. Change your clothes, take a quick walk, do whatever signals to your brain that it's time to switch off "work mode."*

2. Prioritize What Actually Matters

Here's a secret: not everything is equally important. You can't do everything, and that's okay. The trick to work-life balance is learning to prioritize what really matters and ditch the rest. Make a list of your top priorities for the day and focus on knocking those out. Everything else? It can wait.

3. Don't Forget to Play

Life's too short to work all the time. Seriously. Make sure you're making time for fun, whether that's hanging out with friends, playing video games, or just binge-watching your favorite show. **Play** is just as important as work when it comes to managing stress and staying sane.

Tip: *Schedule fun into your day like you would any other task. Treat it like a meeting with yourself, and don't skip it. Trust me, future you will thank you for it.*

Final Thoughts: Chill Without Checking Out

Managing stress isn't about pretending it doesn't exist or bailing on all your responsibilities. It's about recognizing when it's creeping up, using quick, effective techniques to deal with it, and making sure you're balancing your work with your life. **Guys**, don't bottle it up until you explode, and **girls**, don't let stress turn you into a ball of anxiety. Find what works for you, whether it's deep breathing, walking, or a solid laugh, and take care of yourself.

Stress might be unavoidable, but turning into a stressed-out zombie? That's optional. So, take a deep breath, crank up your favorite song, and remember, you've got this.

Chapter 11: Relationships, Building Healthy Connections

Alright, buckle up, because we're about to dive into the wild world of **relationships**, from friendships to romance and everything in between. Let's be real, relationships can be awesome... until they're not. Whether you're trying to keep the drama to a minimum with friends, figuring out how to maintain your boundaries without becoming a hermit, or wondering what a healthy relationship actually looks like, Uncle Aaron's got your back. Get ready for some real talk on how to build and maintain solid, drama-free connections.

Navigating Friendships and Romance Without Drama

Let's start with a truth bomb: **all relationships require effort**, but they shouldn't feel like you're running an emotional marathon every day. Friendships and romance, while different, share a common thread: communication, respect, and knowing when to step back before things spiral into drama central.

1. Friendships: Quality Over Quantity

There's this weird pressure to have a million friends, especially in the social media age where your value is measured in followers and likes. But here's the deal: **it's better to have a few solid friends** who genuinely have your back than 100 people you can't really count on.

Tip: *Don't stress about being friends with everyone. Focus on building strong relationships with the people who actually care about you. The ones who text back, show up, and don't flake on plans. The fewer, the better. Trust me, it's easier to manage and way less drama.*

2. Romantic Relationships: Let's Get Real

Romantic relationships can be tricky, especially if you're diving into them without a life jacket. Here's the truth: no relationship is perfect, and anyone who says theirs is lying or living in a movie. But a *healthy* relationship? That's where the magic is.

First, avoid making your partner the center of your universe. You know what I'm talking about, the kind of relationship where you ditch your friends, hobbies, and even Netflix binge time because you're too wrapped up in being "couple goals." That's a one-way ticket to co-dependency, my friend.

Tip: *Keep your own life, goals, and interests. Relationships work best when you're two whole people choosing to be together, not when you lose yourself in the process.*

How to Maintain Boundaries Without Losing Friends

Let's talk **boundaries**, aka the invisible lines that keep you from losing your mind. Whether it's with friends, family, or a significant other, boundaries are how you keep your relationships healthy. They help prevent resentment, burnout, and unnecessary drama.

1. Say "No" Without the Guilt

We've all been there, saying "yes" to things we don't want to do just because we're afraid of hurting someone's feelings. But here's the deal: saying "no" doesn't make you a bad person; it makes you a person who values their time and energy.

If your friend asks you to go out for the third night in a row and you'd rather Netflix and nap, say it. If your significant other wants to hang out but you've had a long day and just need some alone time, let them know. Boundaries are about protecting your mental health, not pushing people away.

Tip: *Practice saying "no" in small situations first. It'll get easier with time, and your real friends will respect you for it. If they don't? Well, that's a red flag you don't want to ignore.*

2. Speak Up Early

You know what's worse than setting boundaries? Not setting them and then getting mad when people cross lines they didn't even know existed. Don't wait until you're ready to explode before you tell your friend or partner that something's bothering you. Speak up *early* and *often*.

Tip: *Use "I" statements when you're setting boundaries. Say things like, "I need some space to recharge tonight," or "I'd appreciate it if we could text less during work hours." This way, it's* *not about what the other person is doing wrong, it's about what you need to keep things balanced.*

3. Boundaries Aren't Walls

Boundaries aren't about cutting people off or shutting them out; they're about maintaining your sanity while still showing up for the people who matter. The key is to find a balance between protecting your own peace and being there for your friends and loved ones.

Uncle Aaron's Wisdom: *Healthy boundaries make relationships stronger, not weaker. If someone reacts poorly to your boundaries, they might not be the right fit for your life.*

What Healthy Relationships Actually Look Like

So what does a **healthy relationship** even look like? Here's a hint: it's not just sunshine and butterflies 24/7. Healthy relationships are about mutual respect, trust, communication, and the ability to grow, together and separately.

1. Trust Is the Foundation

You can't have a healthy relationship without **trust**. Period. Whether it's your best friend or your romantic partner, trust is non-negotiable. If you constantly feel like you need to check up on someone, or if they're making you feel guilty for hanging out with other people, that's a problem. In a healthy relationship, you don't have to question whether the other person has your back.

Tip: *If you're dealing with trust issues, talk about them. Don't let suspicions fester into full-blown drama. And if you can't trust someone no matter how hard you try? It might be time to re-evaluate the relationship.*

2. Communication Isn't Optional

You've heard it a million times because it's true: **communication is key**. In healthy relationships, you should be able to talk about anything, your feelings, your needs, your frustrations, without fear of being judged or dismissed.

But let's be real, communication isn't just about talking. It's about **listening**. And I mean really listening, not just nodding while you wait for your turn to speak. In a healthy relationship, both people listen and try to understand each other's perspectives.

Tip: *Have regular check-ins with your friends or partner. It doesn't have to be a full-on therapy session, but making space to ask each other, "How are we doing?" can go a long way in keeping things healthy.*

3. You Support Each Other's Growth

Healthy relationships are like a good workout. They challenge you, push you, and make you stronger. If someone's holding you back, keeping you from chasing your goals, or making you feel small? That's not healthy.

In the right relationships, your people will cheer you on, support your growth, and encourage you to be the best version of yourself. And it goes both ways. You should be able to root for your friends and partner as they pursue their dreams, even if it means you're spending a little less time together.

Tip: *Growth isn't a competition. If your friend lands a big job or your partner crushes a new hobby, be happy for them. Your success doesn't take away from theirs, and theirs doesn't take away from yours.*

Final Thoughts: Building Healthy Connections

Building and maintaining **healthy relationships** takes work, but it's totally worth it. Whether it's with friends, family, or a romantic partner, the key is finding balance, setting boundaries, and communicating openly. **Guys**, don't be afraid to talk about your feelings or set boundaries when you need them. **Girls**, remember that healthy relationships help you grow and thrive, they don't hold you back.

The people you surround yourself with have a huge impact on your life. Make sure those relationships are healthy, supportive, and free from unnecessary drama. And when in doubt? Just remember that a solid friendship (or relationship) is built on trust, communication, and the ability to laugh at each other's bad jokes.

-- 111 --

Chapter 12: Career Prep, How to Nail the Adulting Game

So, you're stepping into the real world, and the idea of "career prep" is lurking around like that final boss in a video game you're not ready to face. But guess what? **Adulting** doesn't have to be a nightmare. With a few tricks up your sleeve, you'll be out there crushing job interviews, building a resume that screams "hire me," and planning your career like a pro. And no, you don't need a PhD in Adulting to figure it out. Let's dive into how to play the career game, and win.

Building a Killer Resume Before You've Got Much Experience

If you're thinking, "But Uncle Aaron, I haven't done anything impressive yet. How can I make a resume that stands out?" Relax. No one expects you to have cured cancer by the time you're 22 (though, that would be impressive). The key to a killer resume isn't about padding it with fake achievements; it's about highlighting the skills and experiences you *do* have.

1. Make What You've Got Look Good

Just because you're not a CEO doesn't mean you don't have skills. Have you volunteered? Worked a part-time job? Helped organize a community event? All of that counts. Employers want to see that you've been doing *something* and that you've picked up real-world skills along the way, things like teamwork, problem-solving, and communication.

Tip: *Use action verbs to make everything sound better. Instead of saying "worked at a pizza shop," say "managed customer orders and provided excellent service." Suddenly, you sound like a pro.*

2. Focus on Transferable Skills

Even if you haven't had a lot of formal work experience, chances are you've developed skills that will impress an employer. **Transferable skills**, like leadership, time management, and organization, are gold on a resume. These are the things you can carry with you into any job.

3. Don't Forget to Customize

One resume does *not* fit all jobs. You need to tweak it depending on the job you're applying for. Look at the job description, see what they're asking for, and make sure your resume reflects the skills and experience that match. It's like playing dress-up with your resume to make it look like the perfect fit for each gig.

Job Interviews: What to Say and What to Leave at Home

Interviews can feel like being in the hot seat of a game show where the prize is your future. But don't sweat it; job interviews are just conversations with a little more pressure. Knowing what to say (and what not to say) is half the battle.

1. The First Rule: Be Yourself, But the Polished Version

Interviews are not the place to show off your talent for doing celebrity impressions or ranting about how much you hated your last job. You want to come off as professional, confident, and, well, **someone they want to work with**. That doesn't mean being a robot; it means being yourself, but the *professional* version of yourself.

Tip: *Practice with a friend or in front of a mirror. Get comfortable talking about yourself without sounding like you're bragging or underselling your abilities.*

2. Talk About Your Skills, Not Your Ego

When they ask about your experience, focus on what you learned and the skills you've gained. Employers want to hear about how you can bring value to their company, not how you single-handedly saved your last workplace from total destruction.

Tip: *Use the STAR method (Situation, Task, Action, Result) when talking about your experiences. It shows that you not only tackled a challenge but also got some solid results.*

3. The Tricky Questions

You know they're coming: the dreaded "What's your biggest weakness?" or "Tell me about a time you failed." The trick here is to be honest but strategic. Don't say, "I have no weaknesses" (they'll know you're lying), and don't pick something that's a huge red flag. Choose a weakness that you're actively working on, like "I used to struggle with time management, but I've started using task management tools to stay on top of things."

Tip: *Leave personal baggage at home. They don't need to know about that terrible breakup or your fear of spiders. Keep it relevant to the job and your skills.*

Long-Term Career Planning: It's Not as Scary as You Think

Long-term career planning sounds like something only overachievers worry about, but here's the truth: **it's not as scary as it sounds**. You don't need to have your entire life mapped out, but having a rough idea of where you want to go and what steps you need to get there will save you from wandering aimlessly through job after job.

1. Set Short- and Long-Term Goals

Start by setting **short-term goals** (like getting that entry-level job) and **long-term goals** (like becoming a manager in five years or owning your own business). The key is to make sure your short-term goals feed into your long-term ones.

Tip: *Think of your career as a ladder. Each job or opportunity is a step up. You don't need to leap to the top right away, just focus on getting to the next rung.*

2. Don't Be Afraid to Pivot

Here's the thing about career planning: it's not set in stone. Maybe you'll get a few years into a job and realize it's not what you want. That's okay. You can always pivot, change industries, or pursue new interests. The important part is learning from each step and building skills that will help you wherever you go.

Tip: *Keep learning. Whether it's taking online courses, attending workshops, or just reading industry blogs, always be expanding your skillset. The more you know, the more options you'll have down the line.*

3. Build a Network (Without Being Cringey)

The old saying, "It's not what you know, it's who you know" still holds true. Building a **network** of people in your field can open doors you didn't even know existed. But here's the catch: don't be that person who only reaches out when they need something. Build genuine relationships with people in your industry.

Tip: *Start small. Connect with colleagues, attend industry events, or even join relevant groups on LinkedIn. Networking doesn't have to be awkward if you approach it with authenticity.*

Final Thoughts: Crushing the Career Prep Game

Building your career might feel like climbing Mount Everest, but with the right tools and mindset, you can get there, one step at a time. **Guys**, don't freak out if you don't have tons of experience. Focus on the skills you've got and make them work for you. **Girls**, don't be afraid to step up and take charge of your career path, you've got everything you need to make it happen.

In the end, it's all about positioning yourself to succeed, whether that's nailing your resume, acing interviews, or mapping out your long-term goals. Adulting might be hard, but with a little bit of strategy (and maybe a lot of coffee), you're going to crush it. Now go get that job!

Chapter 13: Structured Techniques

Mindfulness & Emotional Intelligence

Let me tell you a quick story to set the scene: imagine you're juggling work, school, and trying to have a social life. It's not exactly a *Zen* existence. You're overwhelmed, anxious, and probably feeling like you're one email away from losing it. Sound familiar? Now, imagine being able to step back, take a deep breath, and re-center yourself before things spiral out of control. That's the magic of **mindfulness** and emotional intelligence (EQ), and trust me, once you learn these skills, life becomes a whole lot more manageable.

You see, mindfulness and EQ aren't just buzzwords thrown around by yoga instructors or therapists, they're crucial tools for anyone who wants to navigate life with less stress and more clarity. These techniques aren't about being "chill" all the time, either; they're about developing self-awareness and building the ability to manage your emotions, even when life is chaotic. They help you stay cool under pressure, respond rather than react, and foster better relationships with others. In this chapter, we'll dive into **mindfulness techniques** and **emotional intelligence training**, two essential skills that will keep you grounded and help you understand both yourself and the people around you.

Why Mindfulness Matters

Mindfulness is essentially the practice of being present. It's about **being aware** of what's happening in the moment without getting caught up in it. Ever notice how your brain is constantly on overdrive, thinking about what's next on your to-do list, or replaying awkward moments from the past? That's what mindfulness helps with, it quiets the noise.

Incorporating mindfulness into your daily life can improve focus, reduce anxiety, and even improve sleep. Plus, when you're mindful, you can respond thoughtfully rather than react impulsively to situations. This means fewer "What was I thinking?" moments and more "I handled that well" moments.

Example: *Let's say you get an angry text from a friend. Without mindfulness, your first instinct might be to shoot back a snappy reply or escalate the argument. With mindfulness, though, you pause, acknowledge your emotions, and think about how you want to respond. You're not avoiding the problem; you're addressing it with a clearer head.*

Mindfulness Techniques: How to Practice Daily

Let's get into the practical side, how you can apply mindfulness every day. It doesn't have to be a major time commitment; even five minutes a day can make a difference.

1. Guided Body Scans

A body scan is a mindfulness technique that helps you get out of your head and into your body. It's a great way to reduce tension and connect with yourself. Here's how it works:

- Find a quiet space where you won't be interrupted.

- Close your eyes and start by focusing on your toes. Slowly move your attention up your body, noticing any areas of tension.

- Breathe deeply into each area. If you find a tight spot, like your shoulders, take an extra moment to breathe into it, allowing it to relax.

- By the time you've worked your way up to your head, you'll feel much more grounded and aware of your body.

Why it's important: *Most of us carry tension without even realizing it. Doing a body scan daily can help you check in with your body and release built-up stress before it turns into a headache or muscle strain.*

2. Mindfulness Check-ins

A mindfulness check-in is a simple yet powerful practice that only takes a couple of minutes. The idea is to pause throughout your day, check in with yourself, and ask, "How am I feeling right now?"

- Set an alarm on your phone to go off three times a day as a reminder to check in with yourself.

- When the alarm goes off, stop what you're doing and take a deep breath.

- Ask yourself: "What's on my mind right now? Am I stressed, happy, anxious?"

- Don't try to fix anything, just acknowledge where you are mentally and emotionally.

Why it's important: This practice builds self-awareness, which is key to emotional regulation. When you know how you're feeling in the moment, it's easier to make intentional choices rather than letting emotions control you.

3. Breathing Techniques for Stress

When things get chaotic, your breath is your best friend. Practicing deep breathing helps calm your nervous system and get you back into the present moment. One effective method is the **4-6 Breathing Technique**:

- Inhale for 4 counts.

- Hold for 1 count.

- Exhale for 6 counts.

- Repeat for at least one minute.

Why it's important: *Breathing exercises like this help lower your heart rate and cortisol levels, the hormones associated with stress. When you're calm, you can think more clearly and make better decisions.*

The Power of Emotional Intelligence

Now that you've got mindfulness down, let's talk about **emotional intelligence**, or EQ. Emotional intelligence is all about understanding and managing your emotions and being able to recognize and influence the emotions of others. It's a key factor in developing strong relationships, both personally and professionally.

Emotional intelligence has four main components:

- **Self-awareness**: Knowing what you're feeling and why.

- **Self-management**: Handling your emotions in a healthy way.

- **Social awareness**: Understanding how others are feeling.

- **Relationship management**: Navigating relationships effectively.

EQ is often more important than IQ when it comes to success. Why? Because you can be the smartest person in the room, but if you can't control your emotions or connect with others, you'll struggle to lead or collaborate effectively.

Emotional Intelligence Training: Key Practices

Let's break down how you can build emotional intelligence.

1. Identifying Emotional Triggers

The first step to managing emotions is understanding what triggers them. Think back to the last time you felt angry, frustrated, or even overly excited. What set you off? Was it something someone said? A specific situation?

- Create a trigger journal where you write down situations that caused an emotional reaction. Identify the trigger, your reaction, and how you handled it.

- Over time, you'll notice patterns and can work on responding differently to situations that typically throw you off balance.

Why it's important: Once you know what triggers your emotions, you can anticipate them and manage your response, preventing impulsive reactions that could harm your relationships or well-being.

2. Practicing Active Listening

Communication isn't just about talking; it's about **listening**, too. Active listening means fully focusing on the person speaking, not just waiting for your turn to talk. Here's how to practice it:

- When someone is talking to you, focus on their words rather than thinking about your response.

- Nod, make eye contact, and use small verbal acknowledgments like "I see" or "Go on" to show that you're engaged.

- After they finish, summarize what they said in your own words to show you understood.

Why it's important: Active listening helps you connect with others and shows that you respect their feelings and opinions. It's crucial for building trust and understanding in any relationship.

3. Empathy-Building Exercises

Empathy is the ability to understand and share the feelings of another person. It's what allows you to connect on a deeper level and respond with compassion rather than judgment.

Try this: *Think about a recent conflict or misunderstanding you had with someone. Now, imagine the situation from their perspective. How do you think they felt? What might have motivated their actions? Write down your thoughts and reflect on how this new perspective changes your view of the situation.*

Why it's important: Empathy builds stronger relationships. When you can step into someone else's shoes, you're less likely to jump to conclusions or make things worse during a conflict.

The Importance of These Techniques in Everyday Life

Both mindfulness and emotional intelligence are **game changers** when it comes to navigating stress, relationships, and life's challenges. Think of them as your mental and emotional toolkits. When you practice these techniques regularly, you're better equipped to handle whatever life throws your way, whether it's a demanding boss, an argument with a friend, or just a hectic day.

The truth is, life is full of unpredictable moments. You can't control everything that happens to you, but you can control how you respond. Mindfulness gives you the **clarity** to see situations as they are, while emotional intelligence helps you **understand** and manage your feelings and the feelings of others.

Conclusion: Putting It All Together

Here's the deal: **Mindfulness** and **emotional intelligence** aren't magic cures, but they are tools that can drastically improve how you handle stress, relationships, and decision-making. The more you practice these techniques, the better you'll get at managing your emotions and responding thoughtfully to the world around you.

Remember, these are skills you can practice every day, whether you're dealing with a minor annoyance or a major life event. So start small. Set aside five minutes a day for a body scan, keep a trigger journal, and practice active listening in your conversations.

Over time, these practices will become second nature, and you'll find yourself handling life with more ease and confidence.

And hey, if you ever feel like you're losing your cool or you're unsure of what to do next, just remember: take a deep breath, check in with yourself, and approach the situation with curiosity and compassion. Uncle Aaron's got your back.

Adulting 101: Life Skills for Growing Up

Final Chapter: Uncle Aaron Needs to Make Sure You're Fed

Alright, future life masters, we've covered a lot in this book, but we can't wrap things up without ensuring you're well-fed and ready to take on the world. You don't need to be a gourmet chef to whip up something delicious, nutritious, and affordable. With the **grocery list** I'm about to lay out, plus some basic seasonings and creativity, you'll have the tools to make a wide variety of meals.

Essential Grocery List

Here's what you'll need to create tons of meals without breaking the bank:

1. **Protein**:

   - Chicken breasts (5 lbs)
   - Ground beef (3 lbs)
   - Eggs (1 dozen)

2. **Carbs & Staples**:

   - Rice (5 lbs)
   - Black beans (canned, 3 cans)
   - Tortillas (whole wheat, 1 pack)

- Pasta (2 lbs)
- Potatoes (5 lbs)

3. **Vegetables**:

   - Bell peppers (6)
   - Spinach (1 bag)
   - Garlic (1 bulb)
   - Onions (4)
   - Carrots (1 bag)
   - Broccoli (2 heads)

4. **Canned Goods**:

   - Canned tomatoes (4 cans)
   - Chicken broth (1 carton)

5. **Dairy**:

   - Cheese (cheddar, shredded, 1 block)

6. **Fats & Oils**:

   - Olive oil (1 bottle)

7. **Others**:

   - Avocados (4)

Seasonings and Basic Supplies

You can make almost any dish taste amazing with the right **seasonings**. Stock these basics in your kitchen, and you're ready to season and spice up meals for weeks.

Seasonings:

- Salt
- Black pepper
- Paprika
- Cumin
- Chili powder
- Garlic powder
- Onion powder
- Oregano
- Red pepper flakes (optional, for heat)
- Italian seasoning (optional, for pasta dishes)
- Soy sauce (optional for stir-fries)
- Taco seasoning (optional, if you like pre-mixed)

Basic Cooking Supplies:

- Olive oil (or any cooking oil)
- Butter (optional, for richness)
- Flour (for thickening sauces, or tortillas)
- Vinegar (apple cider or white, for dressing or marinades)
- Sugar (a pinch for balancing flavors)
- Chicken or vegetable broth (for soups and stews)

Recipes to Keep You Satisfied

With these groceries, you can whip up about **30+ meals** that are tasty, healthy, and easy to make. Below is just a taste of what you can do. Keep in mind, not all meals can be made at the same time if you run low on certain ingredients. But you can always switch things up, experiment, and make the list work for you.

1. Chicken Stir-Fry

- Chicken breasts, bell peppers, broccoli, garlic, onions, olive oil.

2. Ground Beef Tacos

- Ground beef, tortillas, cheese, lettuce, avocado, canned tomatoes.

3. Chicken Avocado Salad

- Chicken breasts, avocados, spinach, olive oil, salt, pepper.

4. Veggie Stir-Fry

- Bell peppers, broccoli, carrots, onions, garlic, olive oil.

5. Egg & Veggie Scramble

- Eggs, bell peppers, onions, spinach, cheese.

6. Beef and Bean Burritos

- Ground beef, black beans, tortillas, cheese, bell peppers.

7. Chicken Soup

- Chicken breasts, chicken broth, carrots, potatoes, onions, garlic.

8. Chicken Quesadillas

- Chicken breasts, tortillas, cheese, bell peppers.

9. Rice & Beans

- Rice, black beans, garlic, cumin, onions.

10. Beef and Rice Bowls

- Ground beef, rice, black beans, bell peppers, onions.

11. Chicken Tacos

- Chicken breasts, tortillas, cheese, avocado, onions, garlic.

12. Beef Chili

- Ground beef, black beans, canned tomatoes, onions, garlic, chili powder.

13. Pasta with Marinara

- Pasta, canned tomatoes, garlic, olive oil.

14. Egg Fried Rice

- Eggs, rice, onions, garlic, olive oil.

15. Chicken and Rice

- Chicken breasts, rice, spinach, garlic.

16. Vegetable Soup

- Chicken broth, carrots, potatoes, onions, garlic, spinach.

17. Stuffed Bell Peppers

- Bell peppers, rice, ground beef, cheese.

18. Chicken Pasta

- Chicken breasts, pasta, canned tomatoes, garlic, olive oil.

19. Beef Tacos Salad

- Ground beef, spinach, avocado, black beans, canned tomatoes.

20. Spinach & Cheese Omelette

- Eggs, spinach, cheese, garlic.

21. Roasted Veggie Bowls

- Carrots, potatoes, bell peppers, olive oil, garlic.

22. Baked Chicken & Potatoes

- Chicken breasts, potatoes, olive oil, garlic.

23. Chicken Wraps

- Chicken breasts, tortillas, spinach, avocado, cheese.

24. Pasta Primavera

- Pasta, bell peppers, broccoli, olive oil, garlic.

25. Beef & Potato Skillet

- Ground beef, potatoes, onions, garlic, olive oil.

26. Chicken Fried Rice

- Chicken breasts, rice, eggs, carrots, onions, garlic, olive oil.

27. Cheesy Chicken Bake

- Chicken breasts, cheese, spinach, canned tomatoes, garlic.

28. Beef & Veggie Tacos

- Ground beef, tortillas, bell peppers, onions, cheese.

29. Chicken Avocado Wraps

- Chicken breasts, avocado, tortillas, spinach.

30. Vegetarian Tacos

- Black beans, tortillas, cheese, avocado, spinach.

31. Beef Stuffed Potatoes

- Ground beef, potatoes, cheese, onions.

32. Chicken & Veggie Stir-Fry Wraps

- Chicken breasts, bell peppers, onions, tortillas.

Final Thoughts: Keep it Simple, Keep it Satisfying

Not every meal from this list will be possible if you run out of certain ingredients. The key is **creativity** and **flexibility**. If you're short on chicken, go heavier on the vegetables or switch to a bean-based dish. By mixing and matching, you can keep things interesting while still sticking to your budget. Remember, you don't need a gourmet kitchen or exotic ingredients to make great food. You just need a plan, some basic supplies, and the willingness to experiment.

You've got this. Now, go out there and crush it in the kitchen, Uncle Aaron style!

Bonus Chapter: Dealing with Parents, Empty Nest, Boundaries

Asking for Help, and Navigating Younger Siblings

Let's talk about a special kind of relationship: **dealing with your parents** as you start adulting. Whether you're still living at home or you've moved out, navigating life with your parents can be tricky. They're trying to adjust to their new roles (hello, empty nest syndrome), and you're trying to figure out how to set boundaries without sounding like a rebellious teen again. And then, of course, there's the whole matter of **younger siblings**. Whether you're an only child or stuck in a sibling sandwich, family dynamics play a huge role in your journey to adulthood.

Empty Nest Syndrome: When Parents Don't Know What to Do Without You

Parents, especially when you're their pride and joy (no pressure), have a tough time adjusting when their kids grow up and start doing their own thing. It's called **empty nest syndrome**, and it's real. They've spent 18+ years looking after you, and now they have to face the reality that you don't need them in the same way anymore. But that doesn't mean they're suddenly going to stop texting you every five minutes.

1. Giving Parents Space to Adjust

It's weird, right? You're finally off doing your own thing, and suddenly your parents feel... lost? They might call more than usual, want to hang out a lot, or offer unsolicited advice about everything from your job to your grocery shopping habits. It's a **huge transition** for them, so cut them some slack. They're not trying to suffocate you; they're just figuring out how to adjust.

Tip: Check in with them regularly, but don't feel guilty for having your own life. A simple phone call or visit goes a long way in helping them feel connected without making you feel smothered.

2. Helping Them Find New Passions

If your parents are struggling with the empty nest syndrome, encourage them to find new hobbies or reignite old ones. It could be anything, gardening, taking a class, or even traveling. If they have something to focus on that isn't you, it makes the transition easier. And trust me, it'll save you from constant "So, when are you coming home?" texts.

Tip: *Help them out by suggesting cool stuff they can do with their new-found free time. Maybe even get them involved in a family activity, like starting a family fantasy football league or doing a group hobby together once in a while.*

Setting Boundaries Without Starting World War III

Ah, **boundaries**. One of the toughest things to establish with your parents, especially when they're used to having a say in everything from what you wear to what you eat. But here's the deal: if you don't set boundaries, they're going to keep treating you like you're still 12, and that's not good for anyone.

1. The Art of Setting Boundaries Gently

You can't just walk in and start throwing down rules like, "I need my space, don't call me unless it's an emergency." That's a fast track to hurt feelings and misunderstandings. Instead, approach it gently. Let them know that while you love them and appreciate their support, you also need room to grow and figure things out on your own.

Tip: *Use "I" statements to avoid making it sound like they're doing something wrong. Say things like, "I need time to figure out my own routine," or "I'd appreciate it if we could schedule calls so I can balance everything." It's all about finding balance without sounding like a jerk.*

2. Boundaries Aren't Walls

Setting boundaries doesn't mean shutting your parents out or being distant. It just means putting up healthy limits to protect your space and time. It could be as simple as agreeing not to drop by unannounced or setting a schedule for check-ins. The key is consistency, once you set the boundary, stick to it.

Tip: *Be patient. They might not get it right away, and that's okay. Boundaries take time, especially when you're dealing with people who are used to being heavily involved in your life.*

Asking for Help (Without Feeling Like a Kid Again)

There's no shame in needing help every now and then but asking your parents for help as an adult can feel... awkward. Whether it's financial help, advice, or even just emotional support, it can bring up those old parent-child dynamics you've been trying to move away from. But here's the thing, asking for help doesn't mean you're going backward in life. It's just a part of adulting.

1. Be Honest and Direct

When you need help, just be straight with them. Parents appreciate honesty, and if you beat around the bush or act like you don't need help when you actually do, it'll only make things more complicated. Just come out and say it: "Hey, I'm in a tough spot right now. Could you help me with X?" Simple, clear, and respectful.

2. Offer a Plan

If you're asking for financial help, offer a plan for how you're going to handle it. Whether it's paying them back or figuring out how to avoid the situation in the future, having a plan shows that you're still taking responsibility. And trust me, that'll go a long way in making them feel like they're not just bailing you out.

Tip: *Don't make asking for help a regular thing. Your parents are there for you, but they shouldn't be your safety net every time things get tough. Use it sparingly and responsibly.*

Navigating Younger Siblings Without Losing It

Younger siblings can either be your best friends or the bane of your existence, or both, depending on the day. As you grow up and start adulting, navigating relationships with younger siblings becomes even more of a balancing act. You're out there trying to make your own way, while they're still at home doing their own thing. It's easy for them to either look up to you *too much* or feel like you've abandoned them.

1. Be a Role Model Without Being Bossy

You're the older sibling, which means whether you like it or not, they're looking up to you. But there's a fine line between being a role model and being a second parent. They don't need you to boss them around, they have parents for that. Instead, be a guide. Share your experiences, give advice when they ask, and let them make their own mistakes.

Tip: *Lead by example, but don't hover. Be there when they need you but give them space to figure out their own path. And if they ask for advice? Keep it chill, no need to lecture.*

2. Maintain Your Bond (Even If You're Busy)

Life gets busy when you're adulting, and it's easy to lose touch with younger siblings, especially if there's a big age gap. But staying connected is important for keeping the sibling bond strong. A simple text, a FaceTime call, or even sending memes back and forth is enough to keep the relationship alive.

Tip: *Find common interests you can bond over, whether it's sports, video games, or binging the same TV show. It gives you something to talk about even if you're not living in the same house anymore.*

3. Let Them Grow Up (Without Losing Your Mind)

Here's the kicker: younger siblings grow up, too. And sometimes, that means they'll do things you don't agree with or take paths that surprise you. It's tough, but part of being an older sibling is letting them make their own choices, without trying to control the outcome. Just because you think you know better doesn't mean you get to dictate their life.

Uncle Aaron's Wisdom: *Be supportive, even if you think they're making a mistake. They'll figure it out, just like you did. And who knows? They might surprise you.*

Final Thoughts: Family, Boundaries, and Growing Up

Dealing with parents and siblings while you're trying to figure out adult life can feel like a full-time job. But with the right boundaries, a little patience, and a lot of understanding, you can navigate it all without losing your cool. **Guys**, don't be afraid to ask for help when you need it, but keep your independence intact. **Girls**, set those boundaries early, but keep the connection strong with your family.

Family relationships change as you grow up, and that's a good thing. It's all about evolving together, finding your space while still staying connected. So, set those boundaries, ask for help when you need it, and don't forget to check in on your younger siblings. You've got this!

Wrapping Up with Uncle Aaron's Final Pep Talk

So, you've made it through the wild ride of life skills, adulting hacks, and navigating relationships without losing your mind.

Here's the thing, **life isn't about getting everything right all the time**, it's about learning, adapting, and laughing through the chaos.

Whether you're managing a career, setting boundaries, or just trying to figure out why the universe is obsessed with throwing curveballs, remember that you've got everything you need to handle it.

You don't need to have it all figured out right now. Spoiler alert: no one does. The key is to keep showing up, keep learning, and never take yourself too seriously. **Adulting is hard**, but you've got this, and if you ever feel lost, just think of Uncle Aaron giving you that extra push (or kick in the pants) you need.

Here's your final pep talk:

1. **Stay curious**. Life's a lot more fun when you're learning, whether it's a new skill, hobby, or just how to navigate tricky situations.

2. **Don't fear failure**. Messing up is just a step toward getting better. Learn from it and move on.

3. **Laugh often**. Seriously, it's the best medicine. Don't let the seriousness of life crush your sense of humor.

Now go out there, embrace the chaos, and remember, you're already killing this whole life thing. And if you ever need a reminder? Uncle Aaron's always here with a fresh dose of tough love and good laughs. **You've got this!**

-- 144 --

Author Bio

Aaron B. Kershaw is an author, mentor, and former U.S. Marine whose mission is to empower others through resilience, financial education, and practical life skills. With a diverse career spanning corporate leadership, media production, and community service, Aaron combines humor, insight, and hard-earned wisdom in his writing. His early experience managing a business as a high school student laid the groundwork for a lifelong dedication to helping others, a path that led him to significant roles with organizations like Habitat for Humanity and Guiding Eyes for the Blind.

A licensed financial advisor, insurance professional, and educator, Aaron has guided individuals and businesses through complex financial landscapes, helping them make informed decisions and reach their goals. Known for his straightforward and relatable approach, he focuses on making life's toughest concepts more accessible and actionable. Beyond business and self-help, Aaron also writes teen thrillers, captivating younger audiences with suspenseful, action-packed stories.

Through his books, Aaron inspires readers of all ages to navigate life's unexpected twists, grow from every setback, and build a life of resilience and purpose.